DIANE MEIER DELANEY

the
new
american
Wedding

RITUAL AND STYLE IN A CHANGING CULTURE

Illustrations by Donna Mehalko
Jewelry photography by Ken Skalski

Viking Studio

VIKING STUDIO
Published by the Penguin Group
Penguin Group (USA) Inc., 375 Hudson Street,
New York, New York 10014, U.S.A.
Penguin Group (Canada), 90 Eglinton Avenue East, Suite 700,
Toronto, Ontario, Canada M4P 2Y3
(a division of Pearson Penguin Canada Inc.)
Penguin Books Ltd, 80 Strand, London WC2R 0RL, England
Penguin Ireland, 25 St. Stephen's Green, Dublin 2, Ireland
(a division of Penguin Books Ltd)
Penguin Books Australia Ltd, 250 Camberwell Road, Camberwell,
Victoria 3124, Australia
(a division of Pearson Australia Group Pty Ltd)
Penguin Books India Pvt Ltd, 11 Community Centre, Panchsheel Park,
New Delhi – 110 017, India
Penguin Group (NZ), Cnr Airborne and Rosedale Roads, Albany,
Auckland 1310, New Zealand
(a division of Pearson New Zealand Ltd)
Penguin Books (South Africa) (Pty) Ltd, 24 Sturdee Avenue,
Rosebank, Johannesburg 2196, South Africa

Penguin Books Ltd, Registered Offices: 80 Strand, London WC2R 0RL, England

First published in 2005 by Viking Studio, a member of Penguin Group (USA) Inc.

1 3 5 7 9 10 8 6 4 2

Illustration credits appear on page 234.

LIBRARY OF CONGRESS CATALOGING IN PUBLICATION DATA
CIP data available.
ISBN 0-670-03462-2
Printed in the United States of America
Set in Garamond Book

Designed by David Goodwin, Ben Goodwin and Diane Meier for MEIER

For Frank,

to whom I am very married

and

for my parents,

who taught me how

CONTENTS

ACKNOWLEDGMENTS

A book that attempted to blend the cultural anthropology of market analysis with personal memoir all wrapped in the format of a style book was never going to be a simple concept to sell; but a few people got it right off and they should be thanked, right off, with all the enthusiasm I feel. Publicists Patty and Andrew Freedman "saw" the book before I'd even had it out of my mouth and placed it in just the right hands—that of agent Jan Miller. Jan completely backed me in wanting to hold on to the concept in its entirety and introduced me to my wonderful team at Viking Studio, a division of the Penguin Group— Megan Newman, Kate Stark, Kristen Jennings, and Gretchen Koss. Their support, combined with their guidance and their kindness to me and to all of us here at MEIER, has been duly noted and very much appreciated.

I had cheerleaders and pathmakers all through the process of collecting material, personal histories and advice. Dr. Brian Saltzman led the pack with his infectious way of making my concerns his. Dixie Todd, Andrea Giardino, Averil Smith, Rachel Rosin and Anne Watkins all rolled up their sleeves and generously opened their notebooks and their lists of contacts to help this book come to life.

The many brides and grooms who shared their stories, their pictures and their mementos also became a conduit to more couples, planners, photographers, guests and families who added their voices and gave this book depth and resonance. I thank them all; as I do Ralph Rucci, Rosina Rucci and Ralph's staff at Chado, who always made me feel welcome. Charles Bunstine, Maggie Norris, Zac Posen and his terrific right hand, Caroline Bishop, are to be thanked for their generosity of time, advice and illustration. Amy Postle, of John Dolan's studio, was always a delight and a help, as was John, in both direction and enlightenment.

The support and many kindnesses from Bob and Jo Bauer, Mike Vreeland, Elaine Friedman, Jeff Memoli and Jean Gallo cannot be underestimated; nor can the loving enthusiasm from "The Amys" (Churgin and Attas), their husbands (Gary and

Steven), the Chuginettes, Sally Pritchard, Bonnie Hung, Jan Roberts, Susan and Duke Oakley, Reba Ford-Sams and my brothers, Richard and Gordon.

Ken Skalski's wonderful photographs have graced our ads (and helped us win many an award) for more than twenty years. How fitting that he should be part of this journey and how lucky I feel to be his friend and colleague. The brilliant illustrator Donna Mehalko has also worked with MEIER for more years than either of us may want to admit; and while we have produced many beautiful commercial pieces and shared many happy days, none has, for me, been so happy as the days spent on this book. I thank both of these generous and talented friends for their huge contributions to *The New American Wedding*, and to my life.

As for MEIER, Neil Dennehy keeps the office rolling along and protects me in ways I'll bet I don't even know. He is adored and appreciated every day. Lyndon Mosse's off-center views and humor compete with his loyalty in making him treasured. David and Ben Goodwin add to every-

thing good about this place, from the laughter to the lunch table; but most of all, for their layout and design, where their skill and their taste, their discipline and their talent have put into reality and improved, for this book and for so much more, the ideas that exist only behind my eyes, I do thank them.

What do I say about Frank, who shared and encouraged *The New American Wedding* when it was just that—our own wedding—long before it was ever "an idea" and who read every darned word of text at least six or seven times? I get a chance here to announce publicly what he knows I feel every day—that I am deeply grateful and appreciative of his great care and attention.

And while they didn't live to see a page, there is hardly an inch of this book that was not informed by my loving parents (loving to me and loving to each other), who taught me, through word and deed, that there is nothing in this world more worthy of celebration than the right partner.

INTRODUCTION

WE WERE NOT YOUNG. WE WERE NOT UNTRIED. BUT WE

DID SHARE AN IDEA OF WHAT CONSTITUTES LOVE:

A DAY-TO-DAY, HOUR-TO-HOUR, MINUTE-TO-MINUTE

PARTNERSHIP IN WHICH EACH THINKS THE OTHER

THE MOST IMPORTANT PERSON IN THE WORLD AND ACTS

ACCORDINGLY. EACH OF US HAD BEEN FORTUNATE TO SEE

LOVE BETWEEN OUR OWN PARENTS—AND PERCEIVED IT,

RECOGNIZED IT AND ACKNOWLEDGED IT FOR OURSELVES.

When we looked at the possibility of our life together, we found it filled with potential joys and many, many questions to be answered, not in the least: where to begin!

From my angle, Frank's leap to America seemed enormous—exchanging the wood-paneled clubland life of a London man of letters for pushing an obstinate seventy-pound German shorthaired pointer into New York City taxicabs; or swapping his beloved and thoughtful broadcasts on the BBC for sprinkling coyote urine around a New England garden.

Despite the gluttonous deer, the wily coyotes and our unreliable rural-telephone service, Frank fell in love with America. He embraced its energy and opportunity and found it welcoming and beautiful, and, if you can believe it, infinitely more polite than England. He loved the weather and the vistas—from New England farmland to the long-shadowed spectacle one gets looking up Park Avenue at the end of a beautiful day. He loved the food—from Maine lobsters and hamburgers to Jean-George and Le Cirque. He loved the music—bluegrass and Motown, cabaret and Bob Wills. He loved the way people on the street—strangers—made way for him, held a door or complimented us on our dog. In short, from the moment he arrived, he was celebrating every day in America.

We had long decided that we should marry and, for many reasons, wanted it to happen sooner rather than later. The shadow of 9/11 had fallen dark across our lives and the phrase "Life is fragile" came too often to our lips. Quite separate from a wedding, I had wanted to create an event to welcome him

this page:

Frank's house

in Somerset, England

opposite page:

Frank and me on our

wedding day

to his newfound land. I wanted a celebration that would surround him with the community of friends and family that made up my life and had offered me the support and love I knew would be extended to him. Perhaps combining the American welcome with the wedding made sense.

Our conversations about the wedding were long and real as we explored every possible kind of option—from a quiet, private, getaway just for two to a family-only ceremony and lunch at home to a destination wedding in a castle in Ireland. These talks were freewheeling and full of laughter—but equally full of honesty, insight, common sense and care.

What became clear in talking the subject through was that we wanted exactly the same kind of event. We had the same values in this as in so many other things and hoped to create a celebration for and about our families and friends that felt unpretentious, very American and full of fun.

When all of the options had been thought

this page:

Coco and me;

Frank's BBC tags

opposite page:

illustrations of Coco

by Donna Mehalko

I TALKED ENDLESSLY TO FRANK ACROSS THE ATLANTIC WHILE WATCHING THE DOG STALK CHIPMUNKS.

this page:

our house in

northwest Connecticut

opposite page:

me on the porch

through, we both came to the same conclusion at the same time: that the front porch of my farmhouse in Connecticut was the place we both loved most—a fact that made it romantic and right. It was the spot where, for hours on weekends, I talked endlessly to Frank across the Atlantic while watching the dog stalk chipmunks. And years before I ever hoped Frank would join me, I'd made a quiet ritual of sitting on that porch at the end of the day, watching the sun set over the mountain that sheltered the Housatonic. It was on that porch that I'd found a way to be quite content in a family that consisted of only, as Caroline Knapp has named it, "a pack of two"—a girl and her dog.

Frank had different, but equally direct, associations with this same porch. On his first visit to Kent he had climbed its steps on a cold November night to see the fires light the facing walls of the dining room and living room as he approached the front door and a New England welcome from my friends and neighbors. And after the terrorist attack of September 11, as we sat there and talked about our future, the porch had become a shelter in the face of what seemed to be a newly precarious world.

And so, we agreed, the porch it would be! But that's all I knew; we would marry on the porch. From that point on I was in a tumult of wedding options, many of which had little to do with us or with our lives. Nearly all of the traditions and much of the information I could find on weddings was geared for the twenty-one-year-old bride and groom and simply not appropriate for someone of our age or someone of our life-experience. I was thrilled to be getting married to Frank. I was looking forward to sharing the day with my friends. But I was not so blushing a bride, and I could see that following many of "the wedding rules" made almost no sense. I looked for direction but found I was on my own; there were questions at every junction.

I was so aware of the fact that I was not The Bride I was reading about in every reference book. "The father usually walks The Bride down the aisle," the book said. "If The Bride's father is deceased, perhaps—" and yes, my father had died twenty years before, but that brought up the whole issue of being "given away."

And how many options were there for an invitation that was not traditional? And what kind of ceremony might include our combined families? And what, in heaven's name, was I to wear?

I was confronted on every page with the fact that I wasn't That Bride. I was something different. If a June bride is the traditional, young, fresh, untried little princess, then, perhaps, I was a Sep-

tember bride—quite literally—September fourteenth and, figuratively, not a June bride; not dew cheeked and innocent. But I didn't feel less than because of it. In fact, I felt quite the opposite.

About the same time I realized that there was no one out there to help point the way, it began to dawn on me that I wasn't alone. While we hear that finding true love after thirty is a lottery with decreasing odds, I was finding this untrue. In the community of women I knew, friends were marrying the men they'd lived with for years, others were finding their own true loves. It might not have been the flurry that surrounded the years after graduation, but just with my outstretched arms I could touch the women I knew were also September brides.

At first I thought it was about age and innocence. And then I sat next to the daughter of a friend at dinner and she turned to me and asked for details about my wedding. It was difficult, she said, to try to plan anything that didn't make her out to be a kind of costumed princess in a phony pageant. I was astounded. Here was a girl in her twenties—albeit a graduate of a good business school with a great career started, but still, a very young woman. Maybe this wasn't about age.

I spoke to another friend soon after, and we filled one another in on the things that had happened to us in between far too infrequent meetings. Her daughter was about to be married, she explained with delight, to a young man who was Japanese American. Her daughter was struggling—though it now seemed she'd cracked the code—on how to craft a ceremony that might be equally respectful of both Christian and Buddhist faiths. The old rules weren't applying.

THE NEW AMERICAN WEDDING ISN'T ABOUT AN AGE. IT'S A STATE OF BEING SELF-AWARE AND SELF-DETERMINING.

A conversation about new rituals began to dominate our social life, and the stories poured in. Couples of all ages were trying to make sense of blending their families. Brides and grooms were looking in all directions for new ways to express themselves, their values, their style, their attitudes, their families, their religions, their lives. There was a lot of frustration out there... and a lot of potential.

It was becoming obvious to me that we needed a new set of options. We needed a way to approach this celebration of marriage with a clear eye to what our culture and our lives had, in fact, become. I was confident I'd find a way to new rituals with no sense of apology for what we were not but, rather, a position of delight and pride in what and who we are.

Once I opened my eyes, it was plain that all around me were New American Weddings. They've snuck in, under the wire, untrumpeted by media, undiscovered by marketers and unnoticed by most of us. And the biggest shame in this is that those of us who'd managed, by hook or crook, to change the ritual to some degree, had no easy way to put out a hand to others and share what we'd learned. We hadn't told anyone of the pitfalls and the mistakes, the fearful, the frightened and the resistance we'd encountered, or of the triumphs and the small and great joys of creating an event as personally relevant and authentic as possible.

Here's what I've found: *The New American Wedding* isn't about an age. It's a state of being self-aware and self-determining. New American couples aren't blushing and they aren't representing their parents' social or economic standing; in fact, they're standing on their own, celebrating the partnership of two fully realized and unique individuals. They are integrating and blending families past and present, careers and homes, pets, plants, cultures, religions, standards and status into an event of practical negotiation, romantic optimism and pure joy. A New American Wedding isn't a cookie-cutter icon-laden rehash of tradition. It expresses the

the porch dressed for the wedding; Frank and me

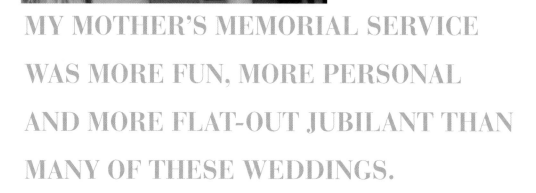

MY MOTHER'S MEMORIAL SERVICE WAS MORE FUN, MORE PERSONAL AND MORE FLAT-OUT JUBILANT THAN MANY OF THESE WEDDINGS.

this page:

my bouquet by Zeze

opposite page:

Frank and me

photographed at the

"studio in the field"

at our wedding

union of two grown-ups in unique and honest ways and celebrates the depth of the couple's relationship as well as the breadth of their lives.

Well, that's all well and good, I can hear you saying, but reinventing our most iconic ceremony can't be as simple as it sounds.

No kidding. I know exactly how challenging it was, when planning our wedding, to know what rules

to break, what rules to hold on to and what rules to reinvent—and all without the safety net of a guide. In all the books, from creative to traditional, not one of them spoke to a grown up with the needs and the issues I brought to the table. What I didn't know, I'd find out.

But easy? No one would tell you it was easy. Certainly not I.

No wonder many of the recent brides I'd known had opted out of a big event and staged quiet, reserved ceremonies. They wore pretty tailored suits and had dignified, quiet receptions. Underlying these choices, there seemed to be the idea that a full-blown, "pull-out-all-the-stops" sense of celebration was a little unseemly. Did I sense a hint of shame if the bride was no longer young, if the marriage was not the first for both? If the ceremony didn't fit the couple, was the couple wrong?

I'd been to dozens of these ceremonies and I can tell you that my mother's memorial service was more fun, more personal and more flat-out jubilant than many of these weddings.

I wanted more. We wanted more. We wanted a wedding filled with joy and celebration. We wanted to

rejoice with family and friends and share with them our utter delight, complete commitment and grateful happiness. We wanted a no-holds-barred reflection of the things in our life that gave us the most pleasure and pride. We wanted a day full of meaning and a celebration full of delight.

This wasn't meant to be just any party—and I don't think it should be. This was our wedding and we were the bride and groom. But how do you play icons when you need to reinvent the models? That's what this book sets out to discover and celebrate!

CHAPTER 1

THE PROPOSAL

MICHAEL WEBB, HERALDED ON HIS OWN WEBSITE AS A "LEADING EXPERT ON ROMANCE," ANNOUNCES IN THE AD FOR HIS BOOK, *THE ROMANTIC'S GUIDE TO POPPING THE QUESTION*, "MARRIAGE PROPOSALS DON'T HAVE TO COST A FORTUNE." WELL, SILLY ME. I DIDN'T THINK MARRIAGE PROPOSALS HAD TO COST ANYTHING.

*I*t seems, however, while I was not paying attention, the whole proposal business had turned into a—business! In fact, it is an industry; with hot-air balloon proposals, diamonds-in-the-cream-puff proposals, candle-bedecked gondolas—with singing gondoliers, skywriters, telegrams and scuba-divers for hire—that promise to pop up out of lakes in the moonlight and proffer engagement rings.

The Algonquin Hotel's press agent put out an idea that was picked up in travel magazines all over America: "The Algonquin Wedding Proposal Martini." It seems that for $10,000 they will substitute a diamond engagement ring for the olive.

Maybe I really am too old for all of this romance; all I can think of are cracked molars, diamonds swallowed with whipped cream and a ring at the bottom of a lake. Trust Frank to suggest that the scuba diver might simply swim away with the merchandise.

I found companies that would place proposals in corked bottles with cheesy messages that said things like "There may be days when we'll want to throw in the towel." A book promised to tell me the "four words you should never say during a proposal" and while the ad didn't mention towels, it was almost intriguing enough to get me to fork over $24 for the book.

If that doesn't do it for you, a twenty-first-century John Alden will charge an hourly fee to write a marriage proposal for you. How anyone involved will manage the fact that poetry eloquent enough to win a hand in marriage will have evaporated just a day later is beyond me.

Decidedly less elegant are the Internet greeting cards with his and her underpants hanging on a clothesline that invite the receiver to "Marry Me." And a banner company suggests that popping the question on one of their 14' X 5' banners is "cheaper, at $22.95, than a billboard."

But I don't think most of these proposals apply to the couples we're visiting in *The New American Wedding*. The challenges in the proposals of more mature and more fully developed individuals are not going to be solved by messages in bottles or diamond rings hidden in shrimp cocktails. One of the things I know is that for grown-ups, the course is more precarious. The dangers are real. This is not the time for gimmicks.

Isn't it interesting that a book that asks couples to assume as a primary foundation that the tried and true may not be good enough or fresh enough for them (too tried, and rarely true enough) is reporting on the fact that proposals for our New American group are almost never inventive. And we're endorsing it.

The decision to get married is not to be taken lightly, as the ceremony goes. We stand in the face of broken families, broken promises, broken contracts and still believe that this time it will be different. There are distinctions to these couples whom we identify as being of our New American group. They are more self-aware, more self-assured and more comfortable with the fact that their uniqueness is something to celebrate. Only living teaches you this. And only when you are in a position to see yourself clearly are you able to make the kind of promise you will want to and be able to keep as you grow.

No matter how fast their hearts might beat, the blending of more mature couples (from those in their twenties to those in their eighties) cannot be approached as easily or innocently as new graduates who barely own a suitcase, no less the emotional baggage of a fully lived life.

These grown-up unions often need to be approached with clear heads, strong stomachs, loving patience and the skill of a board of directors merging two Fortune 500 companies in full view of Wall Street.

ONE OF THE THINGS I KNOW IS THAT FOR GROWN-UPS, THE COURSE IS MORE PRECARIOUS. THE DANGERS ARE REAL. THIS IS NOT THE TIME FOR GIMMICKS.

Here we have couples where a woman might make more (much, much more) than the man who loves her and, I might say, than the man she loves. And despite inequities in high management positions, we are just as likely, these days as not, to see a woman with an important job and considerable corporate demands on her time; a woman who simply might not be able to pick up and move across town, across country, continents or oceans to be with the man she loved.

I know of one woman, an executive of a large cosmetic company, who fell in love with one of the photographers shooting their campaign. Falling in love was easy, the decision to commit felt natural. The decision to marry was almost impossible. Because of corporate company policy, if they married, the photographer would lose his largest account or the executive would have to resign. In the end, she kept her job, he found other accounts, they had a baby and all lived happily ever after. But you can see that the issues surrounding the Proposal were less likely to have happened forty years ago.

While the average American story may not be about a cosmetics executive and a photographer, the dilemma is happening all across this country, as top women executives, academics, military officers, board members and public officials meet and fall in love with vendors, teachers and men applying for grants, jobs, favors, recruitment and advancements of all kinds. It's a different world.

Even when there is no conflict of careers, the idea of a woman alone no longer means that she has no options to care for herself. So many of our habits, traditions and assumptions come from a society, not so long past, where a single woman was virtually without protection—financial, physical or social. At some point, she would have to assume that a husband, any husband, would have to be better than living alone. Today, the desire to partner may be strong, but it is now based largely on emotional requirements.

Men, therefore, face a new world when asking women to marry them. Yet we continue to be bombarded with dire facts—like one recently compiled by the universities of Aberdeen, Bristol, Edinburgh and Glasgow that supposedly shows that a "high IQ is a hindrance for women wanting to get married." While men's likelihood of marriage increases by 35 percent for every 16 point increase in their IQ, women's drops 40 percent for each 16 point rise.

Or so says the survey that was widely reported, though given no detailed analysis, in the news. These kinds of statistics beg more questions than answers. Most of all, they throw fuel on the fire of insecurity by suggesting that men want to feel dominant and strong and that smart women will pay for their ambition or their greater talents with loneliness. Our study suggests that neither fact is true.

Our work was informal. With a net not large enough to be scientific, my report is what we call, in marketing, "anecdotal." Directional, but not provable. Introductions made from friend to friend, photographer to client, caterer to florist, bridesmaid to bride. Not the stuff that builds scientific study, but certainly the beginnings of

MANY OF THE NEW AMERICAN WEDDING COUPLES INTERVIEWED HAD GROOMS YOUNGER THAN BRIDES.

ideas that start to pay off in supportive examples as the circle widens.

Our interviews about proposals turned up a number of surprises among them, the fact that many of the New American Wedding couples interviewed had grooms younger than brides; sometimes by only a year or two, in one case by eighteen years. Many of the brides were perfectly comfortable maintaining the relationship without marriage. It was the groom, in many cases, who pursued the idea.

As I've mentioned, a woman who does not feel herself to be "iconic" might put off the idea of staging a wedding, because she feels she has

Jenny Will You Marry Me?

no models, and that may very well play into this mix; but the romance of the groom, his interest in tradition, his desire for connection in the ritual and his need to make a statement about commitment was something that took some of us by surprise. Not Frank, I have to say, but we'll come to that later.

The proposals took place in every possible venue, from bed to car to train. One of our New American Grooms tells us that he turned to his now wife and said something like "I need to know if you don't want to get married or you don't want to get married to *me*." Many of them asked many, many times.

But the vast majority just assumed they would marry. Many have no recollection of either one doing the asking. Most fell into it naturally, like natural couples who belong together. More romantic, to my way of thinking, than the stories of men on their knees, diamonds in martinis, proposals written in airplane vapor, caviar or chocolate mousse.

Whatever the circumstances, the idea of ask-ing risks the possibility of rejection and some-times, in this modern world, with modern women, rejection could simply mean a life that cannot easily accommodate change.

Frank looked at my life, my business, my eld-erly dog and decided that asking me to marry him would have to include his moving to Amer-ica. A writer, he bravely told me, takes his career with him wherever he goes. But, of course, things are never really so simple as taking one's career along to another country. He resigned from more than 120 committees, commissions, boards and clubs and moved from a country where his name was a household word to a country that had never heard of him. I don't know that I could have been as brave as he, but I also know that the idea of life without him might have motivated me to do things I'd thought myself incapable of mastering.

CHAPTER 2

THE BRIDEGROOM

IN ALL THE INTERVIEWS, IN ALL THE MANY

CONVERSATIONS, OVER ALL THIS TIME, WE'VE

UNCOVERED SO MANY THINGS THAT MAKE A

NEW AMERICAN WEDDING JUST THAT—DIFFERENT

FROM THE OLDER, MORE TRADITIONAL RITUALS.

Some of the differences, I'll admit, may be window dressing—a kind of sizzle that illuminates the idea of new behavior and cultural change. And I would argue that some of this window dressing, when seen (and used) as a metaphor for the deeper stuff of life, is not mere fluff. The great experiment of America, the idea of a huge assimilation of cultures and religions, the tolerance upon which this country was founded, has become a reality. If we see this most clearly in our delivery rooms and on our birth certificates, we see its first celebrations across the country in The Wedding. Some of the changes are social—as older or more sophisticated couples are inclined to plan and pay for their celebrations themselves, the choices they make, be they music or dress, vows or venue, are not what their parents would have chosen. Some changes are cultural, as we've noted, when religions or backgrounds blend within the creation of a new family. But one of the biggest changes I found exhibited in New American Weddings was not in the dress and not in the band, not in the venue or the invitation or the ceremony; the real and somewhat surprising change was in the role of The Bridegroom.

In times not so far past, when Eliza's father, Alfred Doolittle, sang "Get Me to the Church on Time," getting to the church was just about all that was asked of the groom. If he was also clean and sober, if his hair was well cut and his pants unwrinkled, if he remembered the ring, spoke out clearly and didn't faint, there wouldn't even be a cute story about him. Was the groom there? He must have been; there was a wedding, after all.

But it wasn't all (or always) the man's fault. The times and the typical wedding culture supported a "useless" image for men. There are a number of possibilities as to why this might have happened and, while some of the explanations are clearly wrong headed, we can see in each reason some level of connection with the culture we hope we've moved beyond. There is, for instance, the idea that women deliberately froze

this page: Mr. and Mrs. Cornelius Denneby on their wedding day, 1949

opposite page: John Long, groom

out the involvement of men, holding (with, perhaps, some kernel of resentment) the fragile reins of the tiny fiefdom allowed them, however unreal and however ridiculous it might be. There is the possibly mistaken assumption, by men, that showing any interest in veils and china, baby carrots and Alencon lace would label them as less than masculine. There is the far more likely position that nothing in their background or exposure would have prepared them to comment on or understand the difference between baby carrots and Alencon lace. And, in the end, there is the fear of participating in the ceremony itself; dressed in clothes that would be neither familiar nor comfortable, saying words they had never said, in language they did not use, in front of a crowd of people, only some of whom they'd recognize. Which would be worse, they might well have worried, speaking in front of those they knew or those they didn't?

There is a well-known adage that most people—male or female—consider the idea of speaking in public more dreadful than death. Add to this the ever-present horror of doing anything that calls too much attention to oneself; and how must the traditional groom feel when the event is intended to do just that, but in ways in which his control is limited or, indeed, absent? Should we stumble upon a rare and confident groom who could bask comfortably in a spotlight, and what does the traditional wedding hold for him, except to present himself, at the proper hour, as a dark suit against which the bride might glow? The very last thing allowed to him was the creation of his own level of radiance. In other words, the traditional bridegroom was shut out by a system that stereotyped men to themselves and to everyone else as, at best, hewing the wood and drawing the water but never plucking the flowers.

Now, with New American Grooms, we've

come from the extreme distance of hands off the process to hands-on concern; from tippling, emotionally disconnected cheeriness to cochairing wedding meetings and directing the bridal coordinator. Today, New American Grooms suffer embarrassment at not being involved. They fear being thought a blowhard chauvinist. And if he wishes to show that his feet are keeping pace with the spin of the western earth, the New American Groom participates fully in family matters—from the wedding day onward. Not to do so makes a statement of cultural, if not emotional, retardation.

The words heard again and again from grooms, as they talked about their planning and their input, their concepts and their attitudes about their own nontraditional weddings, were, "not stereotypical," "not conformist," "not formulaic," "not traditional." Accent on the "not." I was surprised by the force of the point they aimed to make, as if they were each very aware, whether they were twenty-nine or sixty, of the male image they were working to destroy.

It was a stunning observation and made over the entire field of interviews. We can ask ourselves how such a change can happen in so short a time; and we might ask ourselves how a change like this could happen even within the life of a man who has married before, the old way—and now, The New. The particular answers will surely be within the man, but the general answers are to be found within his world.

No one can fail to see that the world we find today has created a different set of social and economic challenges and opportunities from the world of our parents. At its most basic, the moment men stooped to change their baby's Pampers, once as unthinkable as interviewing a wedding florist, the pendulum began its swing. And now we see a number of New American Grooms eager to prove their part in the evolution of the culture.

In the interviews for this book, three basic types of New Bridegroom emerged: The first takes charge of everything—a total and creative drive of the perfect day he envisages as a gift, a grand gesture to the woman he loves and a statement to his community of family and friends, about himself and about his life within this relationship. The second gets into the details—he has strong thoughts on each and every aspect of the event, but sees the tasks as a collective-team gesture, a presentation of "the art of being a couple." There is nothing he isn't interested in, from the dress to the sauce on the side. And in the end, it is impossible to identify any part of the process as being His instead of Hers. A third sees the activities as being efficiently divided. He makes himself available to contribute in the tasks and areas in which he feels most self-assured. He may design the ring or the graphics, he may coordinate the flowers, take on the mechanical aspects of the event or manage the transportation, the installation of tents and facilities or the choice and booking of the music. He doesn't shirk from being a part of the whole but, rather, makes a contribution based on what he sees as his strengths and skills. And even if he has no larger part in many of the artistic choices, he does not wish to be (or to be seen as) a groom who simply showed up and succumbed to the boutonniere.

The Old American Groom, if we might call him that, seems to have done just this, and upon arriving at the church had a flower pinned to the lapel of his standardized and rented tuxedo or morning coat jacket. *The New American Wedding* talks about brides wearing all manner of personally resonant clothing to their wedding—from daytime dresses of white wool crepe or red cashmere pajamas to taffeta curtain fabric, fashioned into some kind of apparel. It's natural to wonder if we'll see groomswear going from thigh-high waders to Pirates costumes. From the interviews, I'd say no. Not a single groom dressed as a gorilla or even wore his kilt (though one son did just that). As creative as the brides have been, the grooms have tended to the classic. In many cases, however, bits of creative personality emerged as healthy signs of real life.

Jeffrey Michael knew that he was going to stand in front of a black-and-white movie screen and instinctively (and artistically, as a designer) dressed in gray. His white tie was not a bow and, therefore, more of an intellectual than literal nod to the idea of "white tie" as worn by Fred Astaire, dancing behind him. He looked classically correct and integrated within the ceremony. There were no bells and whistles needed, but he makes the point that no one would have stopped him had he considered them necessary. What is, then, appropriate

groomswear for a New American Wedding? And is "appropriate" an idea that even applies?

Frank reveals no surprises when he says that history is on the side of appropriate dress, as the walls of his professional life have been, indeed, papered with dress codes. When he was a young bank employee in the 1960s, his clothes were directly specified: from Monday through Friday, a business suit of dark gray or navy (no plaids, no browns, no tans, no greens); on Saturdays a blazer or sports jacket was allowed with flannels—and always, on all days, a collar and tie. Breast pocket handkerchiefs were permitted, preferably white. He still has the trainee document: "Socks may not be loud, nor may suspenders. The hair, always neatly trimmed, may not be the conveyance of excessive grease." All in all, it was a code intended to instill an impression of steadiness and sobriety in the minds and hearts of the bank's customers.

Not lost on Frank was the fact that these sober wardrobes seemed to mitigate some less than sober behavior on the part of not a few banking associates. Through their pranks and cranks, their buttoned-up suit jackets continued to command respect and deference. Not a small observation for a young man just starting out.

His next dress code came in broadcasting as, obviously, television newscasting was a matter largely of presentation itself. His bank training helped immensely, though he has one real regret. Some years before he began to work for the BBC, the news was read in full Fred Astaire-evening-suit regalia. We can't help but wonder today if a sense of dignified formality in dress might give the news (or the newscaster) a greater degree of credibility or a greater sense of responsibility for the public welfare. It's an interesting thing to consider, when you have a few seconds to rub to-gether on an issue about which you will have no control, input or effect.

Our wedding was on a porch in the country, and Frank considered all of the possibilities of dress, from formal to hayseed; and, as he says, he was to "perform" between the Dixieland band and the horseshoe tossing contest—not too far from *Oklahoma!* (the musical, not the state).

A tux or swallowtails would have looked ridiculous. Even a formal business suit would have seemed uncomfortably stiff. Frank's compromise: a pair of blue jeans (his first ever) worn with a cream wool crepe dinner jacket, a starched white piqué shirt, bow tie, cummerbund, pocket watch, links and studs of tiny enameled horseshoes, and Amer-ica's gift to men's feet—Top-Siders.

Was he comfortable with his choices? I think so. Was he nervous about making them? Sure—who wouldn't be if raised with a code of dress that told you what kind of socks were going to be considered taboo. For the record, I thought he looked splendid. Too late to change history, we de-cided to get the low-down on dressing up from the best authority we could find. The man Frank respects the most on the art of how a man ought to clothe himself also wrote the best book on the subject, *Dressing the Man*, by Alan Flusser.

NOTES ABOUT GROOMSWEAR
ALAN FLUSSER

Alan Flusser considers the subject of men's dress from all received angles, by which we mean that he pays as much attention to the beholder as the wearer and his illustrations come from Hollywood as well as Savile Row. Mr Flusser, a contained man who answers questions from thought rather than impulse, emphasizes a powerful difference between fashion and knowledge. He makes the point that a wedding is supposed to be a ritual and, therefore, more formal—and quickly balances it by permission of eccentricities. "Formal doesn't have to mean dull"—this from a man who entertains fierce views on uninformed dressing. His plea, not just to bridegrooms, can be summed up as—do your homework and choose your moments.

Learn about the clothes you wear.
Learn where the styles came from, what image they portray and, most of all,
how they are to fit your body and your own personal style.

Be meticulous about tailoring.
The most expensive suit in the world
will look like nothing if it doesn't fit you perfectly.

Stay simple.
If you're not absolutely sure that it works,
leave it off and keep it simple. This goes for every possible kind of accessory,
from pocket squares and patterns on ties to colored or patterned vests and men's jewelry.

Be careful about emphasis.
You may be daring, but choose your moments.
Remember that the attention must go on making the total impression.
No one piece should shout in a lone voice.

If all of this sounds unduly conservative, consider this: his showroom and office in New York gleam like an Aladdin's Cave. Color abounds; his dress shirts include glorious red checks with his neckties stately and dancing all at once. But he cautions us, when looking for new ways to express ourselves in ritual, not to encourage a position of casual style for all, but rather to consider, in this day of Casual Fridays and polar fleece at the office, how very few occasions there are when we deliberately dress up and support any level of formality and glamour.

In his own words: "Occasion dressing must be founded on knowledge of how to wear the clothes. I'm all for eccentricities, but at the same time I regret that so many old traditions are fading away. On a special occasion—on all occasions—you have no more than five minutes to make an impression. The way you dress is a communications tool, it's a language. If you care for the way you speak, you should care for the way you dress."

As you'll see in *New American Wedding*,

though we have our share of country weddings (ours and Stephanie and Bill Arnold's, Debbie and David Bain's), we've found some elegant and creative formal events to counter them and offer the point that personality and individuality may be (but is not always) eccentric or casual. It may even be, at times, quite the opposite. Look at Nic and Matt Bolen's masked ball or Susan and John Long's beautifully dressed wedding in Italy.

But again comes Alan Flusser's point about knowledge. Don't limit yourself to the expected. "Learn what your options are. Between formal and dressing down you may have as many as three, four or five options—a silk suit in cream or a navy wool crepe, all the way down to an elegant blazer with an ascot. And never forget how handsome a tuxedo can be."

If you are in sync with the whole event, what you wear may be expressive and personal, sup-portive and appropriate, all at the same time. And that, I think, is what Mr. Flusser means to tell us. Just like your bride—you will be on display. You will be playing the part of yourself. Be creative, be appropriate to the occasion and true to your own style. Do not shirk your effort to be a perfectly dressed version of you.

As Sarah Morris and Jeffrey Michael warn us elsewhere in this book, creating a unique event requires much more work and much more planning than just going along with tradition. For the groom, it often means a far more hands-on approach to the mechanical aspects of the day. While there are sure to be party planners and caterers milling about, florists and assistants will seem to be everywhere—if you have been an integral part of the team that created the event itself, you will be part of the problem solving that goes on as both the normal and extreme challenges of weather and the gathering of crowds take their tolls and time in displaying their own idea of events. So many grooms we spoke to adopted the role of coordinating with the planner as the first line of defense in meeting the challenges that inevitably appeared in the management of an event.

Of all the venues discussed, we found a strong desire among New American Couples to stage their weddings at home. And while I don't see the organization of logistics as gender directed (female wedding planners have, after all, been dealing with tents and cables, septic tanks and sound systems for decades), I will admit that grooms, especially, became animated when discussing the challenge of logistics. The trials of mud and water, boards and railings, drains and driveways sug-

gested above are only intensified when the problems are in your own garden, your own field or your own bathroom. And if you are a groom, facing the performance of your life, these may be the most comfortably familiar problems to address.

Here are a few tips: Your liability coverage against those who fall down your stairs, topple into your pond or break limbs leaping to catch your bride's bouquet should be discussed with your insurance carrier. There are umbrella policies that cover most of the above and riders that can be added, if you are going to add hayrides, ponies, Ferris wheels, trampolines, pogo sticks, white-water raft contests or even line dancing.

The insurance issues become a vital part of your planning, but none so important as the

responsibilities of alcohol consumption on your property. Your party planner should advise you about the laws and rules in your own community. There is, for instance, a Southern custom, or so we're told, whereby a gracious host offers a covered drink for the road to guests upon leaving—the boozy equivalent of a doggy bag. In New England, this can be met with a ticket, loss of driver's license or even auto impounding. Learn your town, county and state laws and make sure your suppliers follow them.

Each of your vendors must have certificates of insurance—for their tents, their jitneys and their catering issues and equipment. A good party planner will see to it that all T's are crossed and all I's are dotted.

There is, of course, the added social issue, when it is your own home, of cutting off someone's intake. A problem, no doubt, during a Christmas party or any other at-home celebration, when, as the host, you must also behave like a parent. But weddings seem to create a special situation, where the idea of frolic and throwing caution to the wind in your guests is met with your need to be onstage and not always available to behave like a parental host. If you don't have a planner on board, make sure that you have assigned trusted and trustworthy individuals to take on this thankless role. You will be busy being The Groom.

No matter how good the planning, things will become unstuck; a power short here, a clogged drain there. We had guests (musicians, actually) who had difficulty understanding why they couldn't park right in the middle of the reception area. Children of friends clogged up a guest toiletand the water flowed down through the ceiling and into our den. We went on smiling and shaking hands because we had others in attendance to help. Planners see this as business as usual and it's one of the truly great reasons to have them on board, regardless of how creative you are on your own.

If you are, however, plannerless, speed and tact become the currency of the day. Phillip Bruno, for instance, changed the scheme for the wedding ceremony's flowers at the last moment, motivating a florist to work flat out through the night because the proposed arrangements seemed to him inadequate to the occasion and the Louise Nevelson chapel. Great details do not call attention to themselves; they support the whole. Phillip knew, the way one who attends to art must know, that no detail was too small to be allowed to detract from the force of the ceremony and the beautiful setting.

There is, finally, much to be written about how men approach their own weddings. Most rituals, what few events are left to us, are faced as a member of a group, but a man's wedding gives him a unique opportunity to say what he's like in the world. In this evolving pattern of nontraditional weddings, the bridegroom's side-by-side contribution can also show the world what kind of husband and partner he's going to make—whether he has the capacity to be imaginative, cooperative, thoughtful, aware. That, it seems to me, becomes the point; and Frank and I think especially of David Bain, six foot three, built like a fort, gifted with the courtesy of the world, standing in the front of the chapel and introducing his family to Debbie's family in a way that created a greater, richer, fuller idea of family. Together they produced a dignified, imaginative, thoughtful, well-intended service that neither of them could have done alone.

Our own ceremony could not have been simpler: no religious overtones, just the plain language of clear and open promise (followed by many jokes, still ongoing, about the deliberate omission of the word "obey" and to whom it might apply). In this, as in every aspect of the event, we discussed and debated each line, testing every idea. And during the compiling of this book Frank and I have overheard or observed the not dissimilar stories as couples young and not so young shared the details and the process by which they created their own ceremonies. There were wonderful recollections—the references to art and additions of poetry included in Clare Henry and Phillip Bruno's ceremony; the reading from journals at the wedding of Matt Bolen and Nic York, revealing how even at their earliest meeting, they knew this was to be important; dozens of stories, all passionately documenting and detailing the process of personal experience within a recognized atmosphere of social change. All of them crafted as much by the groom as by the bride. Jeffrey Michaels might have said it most clearly when he told us that he was not going to stand up in front of his friends and family and present anything that he didn't feel represented him at his best.

His point stands true; in almost every decision of every wedding we looked at, the groom and the bride were united in the way they were presented and in the creative process that brought them to that moment. The brides might have emerged as the keepers of the scrapbooks, the holders of notes and mementos. They took the lead in pulling out illustrations and telling the story of their weddings, and it was one of the few times we saw any real breaks along gender lines in the behavior of our couples. At the same time, however, the amplified voices of their bridegrooms came through loud and clear as they corrected or em-

phasized a point they thought I might have missed, as they added their own take on the moment, as they took possession or credit for a decision or a creative idea.

Frank's reflection is that the grooms' contributions to their own weddings, as we've encountered them, had a natural, uncontrived quality with a deliberate streak of rebelliousness, born of the generosity with which they entered the event and the fact that they very much wanted to be a part of a changing, evolving, more inclusive culture. Often it had profound results, as with Retsu Takahashi, who shaped his own Japanese part of his ceremony to Fiona Gallahue's Celtic heritage; or of tenderness unto tears—Ron Gold playing the flute as he led his bride, Sara Hudson, and her bridal procession to the altar. Jeffrey Michael's photograph of Cranbrook Art Academy was rear projected behind the wedding party. Not only a beautiful image, it reminded all of a place he and Sarah had in common and held in their hearts as intensely special and as a place where they'd met as children. John Long had lived in Italy, spoke Italian and loved it so much that he took Susan Bednar there to ask her to marry him. So important was it to him that it shaped the very nature of his wedding. David Bain knew first that he didn't want to stand to marry with his back toward his existing family. This emotionally connected response formed the basis of their inventive and creative ceremony.

Every man took a position—a specific, identifiable attitude. No bridegroom I spoke to sailed through the planning or the event, nor did anyone seek to. This unselfishness, this desire to contribute and delight at being involved both informed and thrilled all who re-

ported as guests from such shining days.

This kind of openhearted generosity creates an atmosphere of giving that infects all who participate. I encourage grooms as well as brides to be as prepared as possible; and prepared to be surprised. As much as the couples might have been in control of events, there are stories of brides and grooms surprising their partners with unrehearsed vows, unexpected rings and even a song or two. Men are not left out of this inventiveness any longer, nor are they left out of the rewards.

Phillip Bruno, while overseeing all, remains overjoyed at some of the surprise elements in his own wedding. Chief among these came when Phillip (a man who has devoted his life to art and artists) was addressed as Clare's artist son, Damien Henry, read aloud a portion from a Vincent Van Gogh letter:

"The figure of a labourer—some furrows in a ploughed field—a bit of sand, sea, sky—are serious subjects, so difficult, but at the same time so beautiful, that it is indeed worthwhile to devote one's life to the task of expressing the poetry hidden in them." Out of love for Van Gogh, Phillip had carried that quotation in his wallet since he was eighteen years old. Now, a generation later, a continent away and on the threshold of a new and thrilling chapter in his life, he heard it read to him as a gift by his new wife's son.

"Once upon a time," starts the story. The chance of creating a ceremony that reflects the very personal love story of a couple is not the province of storytellers, religious leaders or even The Bride but of the The Couple itself. Once upon a time is now. We now all have the stories within our grasp, and sharing them wholeheartedly is the

opportunity at hand for men and women alike. Grooms have finally stepped over the threshold to pick up the thread of their own story, weave it into their own lives and thus change society in the most significant, creative and authentic ways.

groom Mat Bogen enjoys his own wedding

CHAPTER 3

COMMITMENT JEWELRY

WHEN WE NOTE THE COMING AND GOING OF CUSTOMS
AND STYLE TRENDS, IT'S EASY TO ASSUME THAT THE
BASIS FOR JUDGMENT OF BEAUTY IS FOUND IN THE
CULTURAL LANDSCAPE OF A SOCIETY.

But this doesn't take into account the things people have always found beautiful, without instruction or status: feathers, flowers, bits of stone—smooth from rivers or glinting with quartz, shells and marble, agate, malachite, lapis, coral, fur, bone, wood. Surely these lovely things were used as tokens of affection and courtship long before they were metals and gems pressed into service as enticement, devotion or admiration. Isn't it obvious that the refinement of stones into gems and metals into jewelry merely advanced and developed the practices of sharing beauty as a gesture that is inherently human, rather than cultural?

In his book, *The Triumph of Love—Jewelry 1530-1930*, Geoffrey C. Munn writes: "From time immemorial, the incorruptibility of gold has symbolized the enduring qualities of true love. Similarly, the colour of precious stones has always been associated with the intensity of passion. It therefore follows that betrothal, marriage and anniversary are usually marked by a gift of jewelry; and the favourite choice on such occasions is the ring, which, with no beginning and no end, neatly extends the metaphor."

Through the illustrations and examples in Munn's textbook on sentimental jewelry, one can see that in times past, the variety and nature of design was far more inventive, more personal and more expressive than most of the options we find today. And while he cites the ring as the perfect symbol of continuous love in his preface, he presents many more examples of brooches, lockets, bracelets and earrings as samples of romantic jewelry.

SHARING BEAUTY IS A GESTURE THAT IS INHERENTLY HUMAN, RATHER THAN CULTURAL.

New American Wedding couples are the first to break a pattern of more than half a century in exploring expressions of commitment in selections of jewelry that are not exclusively limited to diamond rings. And yet, when we look for the most significant contrast between these new couples and their parents' generation or their less sophisticated counterparts, it is in the way they approach the idea of commitment jewelry and how they share in establishing its priority of value and worth within the context of their lives that offers the greatest contrast. If, at first glance, this seems a bit cold-blooded, I think otherwise.

While the traditional procedure for a young couple has the ring presented at the time of proposal, the New American Wedding couple often

discusses and negotiates how to balance issues of style and status, values and value. These are conversations that are not likely to take place among the young, where the groom is advised by jewelry shops across the country, to consider two months' salary as the appropriate budget for an engagement ring.

The line between the cultural nudge and the emotional urge is the horizon of marketing. But time after time I've seen that while we can take the beginnings of a trend and capitalize upon it, and we can find ways to help clients make the most of their part in the development of an idea or a look that is catching on or taking off, we can't make the public buy things, wear things, drive things or eat things that they simply don't want to own, drive or eat.

For decades, the fur industry was kept healthy by what they thought of as their bread and butter fare: the husband-to-wife gifts that ran according to his career clock. A mink stole appeared when the husband was made vice president; a mink coat proved appropriate as he hit his presidential stride, and a sable coat became her grand prize when the CHAIRMAN OF THE BOARD sign was nailed to his office door. In the late seventies, the trend stopped, and stopped dead in its tracks. A friend of mine bemoaned the fact, with the observation that they were "just not making husbands like they used to."

So, what makes a man want to give a woman a diamond ring when he asks her to marry him? I'd suggest that it's the perfect cocktail of a primitive idea, to bestow a beautiful token on the object of one's affection, mixed with a sophisticated piece of popular culture. In other words, men aren't

WHAT MAKES A MAN WANT TO GIVE A WOMAN A DIAMOND RING WHEN HE ASKS HER TO MARRY HIM?

born wanting to give diamonds and women aren't born wanting to accept them. But couples may be naturally predisposed to share beauty and show affection through giving and taking. And jewelry, it would seem, is the current expression of that very natural urge.

Most of the New American couples we've spoken to have taken the decisions of expense, from the ring to the costs of the wedding itself, in stride, as they've balanced everything else in their lives together. It is just

one piece of the day-to-day give-and-take they feel privileged to share. In many cases, these are couples who have lived together or traveled together, and their desire to marry reflects the fact that they already understand and share the same ideals and values. Is commitment jewelry less important in New American Weddings than in traditional weddings or is it more important? I think the answer is—both. But either way, the couple is likely to be in tune.

The first story I heard of a straight-up discussion about an engagement ring came from the most remarkable source. Rachel Rosin was the American liaison of DeBeers and, as such, had helped to set the positioning of The Diamond as a symbol of love and commitment for nearly twenty years. When Ben Rosin asked her to marry him, he stated his intention to buy her a ring. But he understood that few people in America knew more about diamond rings than the woman he was about to marry.

Rachel explained that when one is spending thousands of dollars on a ring, it is usually wise to buy the stone first, and the cost of that stone is set on what her industry has named the four *Cs*: color, clarity, carat and cut. She knew wonderful gem dealers and the best jewelry designers in New York. But first, she had to know the budget; and then came the moment of tact. Rachel had to ask how much Ben wanted to spend. Is there a man so secure who might say that he had never worried about the distance between foolish spending and being seen as a cheapskate? Ben tells the story with a crinkle in his eye. He says he took a deep breath and gave her a number, exhaling only when the amount he'd announced was not met with dismay. No doubt Rachel gave him guidelines. And even more to my point, their values were aligned. She would never have suggested, nor would she have been comfortable with his spending an

Rachel and Ben Rosin

on their wedding day

amount that was out of line with the rest of the life they had outlined together. Rachel would contact a gem dealer and she and Ben met at his office to choose the stone for her ring. The dealer, they told me, rolled the diamonds onto a velvet tray and offered Ben the loupe—a magnifying lens—to see the detail, clarity and cut of the diamond. Ben reached to take it from his hand and then rejected it.

"Are you kidding?" he asked, indicating that the loupe should rightfully go to Rachel.

Rachel is now a consultant to the jewelry in-dustry and works with many a private customer to find the perfect stone, the most suitable designer, or a ring that is a dream come true. Her knowledge and proximity have not dimmed her delight in the objects of beauty around which she spends her life. In fact, I asked her how, as one who had helped to set the very idea of marketing diamonds, her own ring could mean as much to her as a diamond engagement ring might mean to a 'civilian', she looked at me in wonder. "I love my ring," she said. "And I love the man who gave it to me." Nothing was lost in the translation. Even more interesting, I think, is the idea that the conversation, between Rachel and Ben about money and settings and diamonds would have been a very unlikely conversation for a young couple. As much as anything else, it projects the idea that neither age nor sophistication dims the idea of romance in New American Weddings.

We're often told that it is the woman who allows the idea of romance to color her thinking, who makes plans based on emotional response, rather than efficiency. And phrases like "Women mourn, men replace" only reinforce the idea of role playing, where man is the practical but emotionally challenged rock and woman is the gentle but unstable cloud. My interviews did not support this in any way. I saw a balance of care and caring, romance and practicality. The best examples happened when I met both at the same time.

Ron Gold is a musician who sees life like an aria. In other words, Ron is a romantic. The vision of how he wanted to ask the woman he loved to marry him included his being down on one knee, in the loveliest of settings; maybe the sun would rest low in the sky and a breeze would rustle the trees. He imagined he would present his love with a diamond ring and she would be delighted with the proposal, the ring and the possibility of a life-long commitment to him. Ron is also realistic, and practical enough about his beloved and about life to understand that some-

times, even romance needs a little foresight.

Ron recognized that Sara Hudson had strong feelings about her own identity, style and the choices she made in dress and jewelry. The idea of second-guessing her was fraught with danger, and yet Ron wanted Sara to have a romantic proposal as faithful to the storybook promise as possible. He wanted her to have that moment to call her own.

Ron called Sara's sister to explore the possibilities of what kind of ring he might choose for her, and Sara's sister also saw the pitfalls of investing in a ring Sara very well might not love. They commiserated until she devised a brilliant solution: Ron should use their grandmother's ring as a temporary prop and give Sara the chance to have both the romantic proposal and the ring of her choice. And it worked like a charm. To my mind, the greater gift was not in the ring—not even in the ring she eventually picked out—but in the way Ron allowed Sara to know that he understood her so well and loved her all the more for knowing her.

Everything about the wedding of Fiona Gallahue and Retsu Takahashi seems original to me and I'm tempted to suggest that because of their blend of cultures, they were required to look deeply at each symbol of their love and commitment. But the more I know of them, the more I believe that they are simply young people of great depth and honest creativity; and in this, they have lessons for all. In the case of jewelry, with all the options available in the wide world, one might still take just a moment to consider creating something that is truly one of a kind and completely personal. Fiona became engaged with a ring designed by Retsu that celebrated their mix of cultures: Celtic and Japanese. He provided sketches for the craftsman who created

the ring in silver, faithful to the drawings. Retsu's desire to be ingenious and reveal himself with his art is something he understands as part of the gift itself. Additionally, the creation of symbols in his life allows him control and an artistic expression that is fulfilling and Fiona's comfort in appreciating and allowing him to make these gestures is the way she returns the gift.

In keeping with Japanese tradition, Fiona has tucked her ring away as a treasure, rather than a piece of jewelry worn each day.

What a wonderful example of jewelry that transcends tradition by celebrating it.

this page: Retsu Takahashi's drawings for the Celtic-Japanese wedding band he designed for Fiona

opposite page: Ronald Gold

43

Sometimes a ring is not a ring. When we were about to be married, Frank slipped into Asprey's and picked out a number of very beautiful and very substantial diamond rings. A few days later I found myself ushered into the store, faced with an expectant salesman and a tray of rings, each one a skating rink. I don't think that my style in dress is timid, but if I wear jewelry at all, it's the sentimental nature of it that touches me. A tray of big white shimmering rocks felt wrong for my style, and the poor salesman could see his bonus disappearing in my eyes as I announced that none of the sparkling rings, lovely as they were, was right for me.

It was early in our relationship. Frank and I had neither lived together nor shared expenses, and the idea of raising a discussion about something as generous as a romantic gift and as taboo as money was not the most comfortable position; but my practical side won out. I tried to be careful as I approached the question about how much those rings might cost.

Frank burst out laughing and asked who'd "raised me"! And I could see my mother cringing, from wherever it is that mothers look down on us—if only from our imaginations.

I explained my thinking. This was, after all, the first major purchase we would make together, and I thought we should put serious consideration into how we might determine whatever we spend on anything; rings included. In time, we got through the land mine issue about gifts' not being purchases one "makes together" and finally rested with the idea that a great deal of money spent on anything

one or the other might not appreciate fully was not the way to begin a partnership.

As it turned out, the cost of the rings equaled the cost of a fifty-foot Gunite swimming pool, raised on a plateau and surrounded by a high wall of field stones, some big as boulders (the produce of all Connecticut meadows). I'd always wanted a swimming pool at the house, and when it was complete, Frank stepped back and said that the wall allowed him to give me the big rocks of his intent. I couldn't have loved it or him more. We will, forever, call the pool The Engagement Pool.

So much about Ellen Carrucci's wedding to Will Tracey has to do with color, and her ring is no exception to this rule. A pink sapphire ring, created by the Los Angeles jewelry designer Cathy Crimerdy was spotted by the couple at the New York specialty store Bergdorf Goodman.

Bergdorf's (like its sister store, Neiman Marcus) presents a jewelry floor as a treasure trove of designer cases and boutiques, filled with examples of fresh, contemporary jewels in all price ranges. Specialty stores, which maintain a point of view aligned with yours and also present merchandise in a broad enough array to give you a wide variety of examples, are a wonderful place to begin your search for the perfect ring. Trying on as many rings as possible, and realizing that the very thing you thought you wanted is neither flattering nor comfortable is a very important part of the process. Don't take it lightly and don't buy a ring without trying it (or something very like it) on.

In the case of Ellen and Will, they found it in the mix of bold and beautiful color with a smart and contemporary design. The staff at Bergdorf's put them in touch with the designer and they discussed ideas for Ellen's ring. Knowing that it was to be an important ring, Cathy started with the stones and shipped them three pink sapphires to choose from. She also suggested that rather than designing their ring in platinum, as Ellen had requested, the pink stone required at least touches of 18k gold, for warmth. Ellen and Will agreed, and when it arrived, it was clearly the perfect ring. They had made a choice that was not traditional, but spoke volumes about the love of color and fresh, bold style of the bride, who has worked at Condé Nast on some of the top fashion and style magazines in the world.

The idea of spotting a trend in the choice of nontraditional wedding jewelry seemed bigger than the anecdotal information I was collecting. To explore the idea further, I planned a tea with some of the country's finest gem dealers and jewelry designers. All women, they responded as professionals, as style setters and as women—

consumers who love jewelry, beautiful objects and notice the changing tides of style in their markets and in their lives. Their verdict supports our claim that one way or another, this new, sophisticated couple delivers a whole new brand of business for the jewelry industry.

On the surface they're tempted to say that it is mostly a matter of the size of the diamond that defines the more sophisticated market, a point that Carol Brody of Harry Winston affirms; and while it is not the whole story, it certainly is an important part of the story. The large, glamorous, clean-shaped diamond has become the first choice for many sophisticated brides. It is the

shape, not just the size that separates this diamond from the selection she may have made in her youth. Emerald cuts, square and cushioned shapes, all offer more surface and an architectural clean-cut line that is, if sales are an indication, more to the liking of a stylish and elegant bride.

But upon further discussion, it turns out that there are far more trends for this new couple than diamond solitaires. First of all, as these are couples who openly talk about money and how they are now going to manage it together, a trusted jeweler is often part of the discussion phase as a New American couple tests the waters of what might satisfy their individual needs and desires.

this page:

diamond rings from

Alexander Primak

opposite page:

a pink sapphire ring

*T*his bride, our panel tells us, rarely wants the kind of ring she might have chosen at twenty-one. There are obvious trends: as mentioned— larger stones with cleaner lines, multiple stones, colored stones, and paved diamonds as detail or surface.

In choosing a ring that supports a bride's individuality, it's important to note that a ring that rings true to one's personality may not be fashion, but it certainly is style; and that leads us to an important point. The rule to watch here, our panel warns, is to avoid a ring (or any piece of important jewelry) that may be, essentially, a fashion choice and, therefore, won't wear as classically as a more time-tested design.

Tiffany & Co. opens at ten o'clock in the morning. I met Linda Buckley, the director of public relations, and Melvyn Kirtley, senior gemologist, on the main floor, just as their gleaming metal doors were unlocked by their civilized but very substantial guards. Within minutes, there were customers at every counter. Tiffany remains the place where dreams of diamonds and pearls

have replaced sugar and spice for girls all over the world and I could already hear many languages and accents fill the room as we made our way to the second floor—the diamond floor. If we were looking to spot trends at the retail level, this was surely the place.

Mr. Kirtley suggested that I was on the right track with the direction we'd gotten from our panel. But he added that there was also a significant trend in the stacking of rings that might be worn in a variety of ways, alone, or together, depending upon the event or the activity.

Of all the major trends in nontraditional jewelry, the one we heard about the most was the choice of a single ring to act as both engagement

and wedding band. The three-stone ring finds its way to the top of the list as the most popular of these options; either set in all diamond or diamonds mixed with colored stones. Multistone rings were popular in Victorian times and the look has cut a new swathe across the landscape of design choices as marketers encourage lovers to invest in the idea of three stones: for their past, present and future.

Pavéd rings and bands set with diamonds create another opportunity for distinction and style, as do bold, wide bands of platinum and gold with or without the inset of diamonds or colored stones.

Some of these lend themselves to rings for men as well, and it's interesting to note that after many years the trend to matching wedding rings for grooms and brides has been increasingly replaced with more individualistic choices for each.

this page, clockwise from upper left:

diamond and sapphire platinum

stackable bands by Rita Fusaro;

emerald cut diamond set in a

contemporary ring by Bondanza;

textured platinum and platinum with

gold bands from Bondanza;

vintage design platinum and

diamond ring designed by Rita Fusaro

opposite page:

Tiffany & Co.'s extraordinary

internally flawless

blue diamond, surrounded by

white diamonds, in octagonal

platinum setting

The central question I raised with Melvin Kirtley was this: What happens when a woman of distinct reserve and restrained style marries a man of prominence and achievement? How can they balance the elements of status and discretion so that both needs are met? Mr. Kirtley smiled and took from his case one of the most glorious rings I've ever seen. A rare, round blue diamond, set in platinum and surrounded by smaller stones was the centerpiece of a ring, almost vintage in style. No stone was huge; no visible "bling" was invited. And yet for those who

know how rare and extraordinary it is to find a blue diamond at all, no less one the color of a midsummer sky, with all the fire and light diamonds are famous for providing, the worth—close to a million dollars—I was told, would be understood.

And there it was—the perfect metaphor for a blend of sense and sensibility, and one that to another couple might seem contradictory. Wasn't this what made so many grown-up couples more interesting, interested and, in the end, far more appreciative of one another.

Not all wedding jewelry is limited to rings. Alexander Primak, the owner and master of a diamond jewelry business cleverly named after himself, tells a story of a bride who had inherited her grandmother's wedding rings and wanted to wear them for sentimental reasons. "And," Alex adds, "because she liked them. She thought they were beautiful."

Her groom, however, wanted to give her a piece of jewelry that would act as a ring; something neutral and comfortable for wear every day, but elegant enough to be included when she dressed for special occasions. With Alex's help, he arrived at the idea of a narrow diamond bracelet of matching emerald cut stones. It is a spectacular solution, and certainly not for everyone (neither in style nor budget), but you can see how it meets the requirements of providing a reminder of their faithfulness and constancy. Alex suggests that the wife of his customer so loves the bracelet that it only comes off every few weeks when Alex cleans it for her and returns it the same day. Just as his customer hoped, the bracelet acts as a different kind of wedding ring.

this page, clockwise from top left: gold and platinum bands set with diamonds and rubies from Bondanza; three-stone diamond and

tansanite platinum ring from Tiffany & Co.; gold wedding bands for men and women by Sean Gilson for Crowe Jewelry;

diamond and sapphire ring with estate crown setting by Rita Fusaro

opposite page: emerald cut diamond ring and bracelet, set in platinum by Alexander Primak

A century ago the idea of sentimental choices in jewelry were many. On the first visit Frank made to America, after we knew this was a relationship that could be satisfied only by our spending our lives together, he brought with him a very special present—an eighteenthth-century French brooch called a honeymoon pin, of cabochon turquoise and rosecut diamonds. These pins were, perhaps, the forerunner of engagement rings as they indicated a relationship that, while on the path, had not yet fulfilled its destiny.

The idea of the historically tried and true object is romantic to many of us who see the survival of beauty through the ages as a worn and loved mark of honor as it extends the benefit of ensuring a look that might withstand the changing fashions of our own time. An enchanting shop in northwest Connecticut takes its name, Lyme Regis, from an English seaside town with a literary pedigree. Not only did the author John Fowles live there, but it was in this town he set his novel *The French Lieutenant's Woman* and the book spills over with its flavor of travel and discovery. In these sailing villages, a hundred years ago, one could find shops filled with the bounty of world travel and the craft of sailors long at sea.

Today, amid nursery china and blankets from Wales, transferware and ships in bottles, the owner, Elaine Friedman, has built a business of ephemera, unusual Victorian jewelry and unique objects that call out to specific individuals in their own wonderful voices.

She has also re-created a line of jewelry much in keeping with the wonderful items she carries. Original Victorian molds of sentimental jewelry have been used to recast gold rings, pendants, and earrings, all of which carry the images and sayings of love. Hands clasp and proclaim "Forever." Cupid rides a dog and promises "Faithfulness." Her foresight makes what would be rare enough to find at all available to all of us. Orders can be taken for rings of any size.

On Manhattan's Park Avenue there is a store many of us grew up thinking of as a true chest of treasures. In my teens, my nose was perhaps too often pressed to their window as I studied a necklace of carved amethyst drops and filigreed gold, which had once belonged to the Princess Eugenie. I imagined myself grown up and sophisticated enough to wear an exuberant diamond starburst pin or the flutter of an extravagant pavéd Art Deco bow. This is the earliest memory I have of thinking that jewelry was beautiful. Here, in this window, it was connected with history and a time of greater glamour and drama than the era in which I found myself living. There was no better place, therefore, for me to end the search of alternative jewelry choices for nontraditional brides and grooms than the source of my own young fantasies, the purveyor of antique porcelains, handmade silver and estate jewels, James Robinson.

Joan Boening is the president and the fourth generation to take the helm of this unique and

prestigious shop. She apprenticed in Paris at one of Europe's finest antique jewelry houses and has brought her knowledge and her keen eye home to run Robinson's with her father, Ed Munves. Together they've created a setting that is both welcoming and impressive, where you can look through cases of jewelry like pieces in a museum, or take a closer look and handle them just for the delight of it, or you might choose to be tutored on the delicacy and symbolism of early nineteenth-century jewelry versus the bold exuberance of the designs from the 1940s. They've increased their investment in men's jewelry, and the cuff links, studs and stick pins articulate the changes in society through time, but always with a voice of stylish elegance and even a hint of swagger.

Because our own wedding celebration had been planned as a country fair with pies, sack races and horseshoe tossing contests, I had chosen a set

top:

nineteenth-century cuff links of

gold and enamel, commemorate

Frank's wedding on the farm

bottom:

silver and gold cuff links carry the

wedding vow "I am yours,

you are mine, we are ours"—

a wedding gift from Clare Henry to

Phillip Bruno

of nineteenth-entury gold and enamel horseshoe cuff links and tuxedo studs as a wedding present for Frank and he wore them with his tuxedo shirt, blue jeans and dinner jacket. In fact, the idea of jewelry for men is a compelling one for New American couples as the bride is just as likely to offer a trinket or two as gifts to her groom. Regardless of who is giving and who is receiving, the staff at James Robinson is savvy enough to steer any couple to options unexpected and often one of a kind.

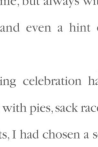

For *The New American Wedding*, Joan Boening understood my quest to present a broad selection of options and chose a number of pieces as illustrations of more personal or unique symbols of commitment jewelry.

If rings are the most likely option, Robinson's has bands of chased metal, some engraved with hearts, and some with knots or bowers studded with precious stones. Delicate choices, like an emerald heart ring, or bold Deco options of diamonds and sapphires, rubies or onyx, illustrate the breadth of style choices all under an umbrella of unexpected and creative thinking. Their wittiest ring is one of their oldest. Lovers' hands embrace; the feminine, handcrafted of rosecut diamonds and sporting tiny rubies as nail enamel; the masculine, of 18k gold.

When we move beyond rings, a brooch in the shape of a platinum knot from the 1920s shimmers with diamonds and rubies and could be made to suggest, perhaps, that a knot has been tied. A pin from the Victorian custom of "Regard" pins, spells out the word "regard" as the first letters of precious stones. In other words: ruby, emerald, garnet, amethyst, ruby, diamond. Regard jewelry formed yet another respectable token of engagement jewelry back in a time of manners, prescribed positions of behavior and symbols of intent. This pin has a tiny sliding glass walled chamber in which to tuck a snippet of the beloved's hair. Another Regard piece from James Robinson is this lovely gold locket with the word "Regard" written out, this time in English.

An Etruscan bracelet of worked gold could be a spectacular signature piece for a woman who is always in some form of sportswear, even when the event is black tie.

right to left:

bold antique wedding bands—platinum with a surface design of hearts, and gold with cabochon rubies and diamonds

Edwardian circle knot brooch of diamonds, rubies and emeralds set in platinum with gold clasp

vintage diamond and ruby ring, set in platinum. All from James Robinson

this page, clockwise from top left:
Victorian gold and diamond ring
of clasping hands c. 1850;
Victorian gold "Regard" locket;
Art Deco diamond and diamond
and sapphire rings set in platinum;
Etruscan-style, Edwardian gold
bracelet

this page, bottom:
"Regard" brooch of gold and
colored stones with tiny
locket for hair.
All from James Robinson

opposite page:
my honeymoon pin of gold,
cabochon turquoise and rose-cut
diamonds

Some of Robinson's pieces carry sentimental engravings, connecting today's couples to lovers from the past. Others have a design that might allow them to create their own, and Joan and Ed will facilitate the process. In fact, they have a client, a man of some substance, who not only loves to present his wife with beautiful jewelry, but he likes to find pieces he can engrave with dates, names, rhymes and thoughts. The mes-

sages and memories they've shared together will be passed down through their family, like notes in very, very beautiful bottles. And so, like most of the direction in this book, there are no hard and fast rules to follow in commitment jewelry, except to follow your heart.

Make choices that speak your language and don't be pushed into "correct purchases" that don't match your style, your budget or your life.

Negotiate the issues of cost and value with one another and be clear in weighing the emotional connection to giving (and getting) against the other things in life you may want or need.

Be careful to choose something that will withstand the test of time and your changing attitudes about style, activities or value.

Open your eyes to embrace the beauty of adornment as though it was meant just for you.

From the feather to the shell to the bit of glass that shimmers in the sun; from rings of diamonds and lockets of gold to pools of water, these are the gifts we choose out of love. They don't hold us together or protect us from harm. They may have no function or symbolism or worth to an outside world, but in the eyes of the beloved they are understood as a kind of stand-in for the messages of constancy. "I will let this gift speak for me and tell you how I feel about loving you." Choose carefully. Make it personal and let the exchange of beauty symbolize all of the delight you find in a world shared with the one you love.

CHAPTER 4

PREWEDDING PARTIES

THE ICONIC PREWEDDING BASH IS THAT DINOSAUR

OF AN EVENT—THE BACHELOR PARTY, COMPLETE WITH

MUD WRESTLING, WET T-SHIRTS OR EXOTIC DANCERS.

ADVERTISEMENTS ABOUND FOR ALL THE MAKINGS

OF A REAL "FUN TIME" WITH INFLATABLE SHEEP

AND ANATOMICAL HATS.

Travel companies hawk Bachelor Weekends in Las Vegas with Playmate tour guides, and the classified sections of city magazines list escorts and strippers with special routines for bachelor parties. It looks like a business to me, and yet not one single traditional bachelor party story appeared in the hunt for *The New American Wedding*, no matter what the age of those interviewed.

Now you might think that no one in their right mind would tell us about a night of revelry when they knew their story might appear in a book. But in all candor, the whole idea of lascivious and adulterous (or is it preadulterous?) behavior seemed to be outside of the emotional vocabulary of the couples we met. There is a kind of approachable maturity to the makeup of these men and women, regardless of whether they are twentysomething or sixtysomething, that goes hand in hand with their self-knowledge and their idea of creating an event of some power and personal resonance, in their own image.

This is not to say that no prewedding celebra-

tions took place. Fathers and sons ate at steak houses and smoked cigars, and many a golf game was had. But for the most part, the idea of gender-segregated entertaining was missing. Conversely, there were no bridal showers—lingerie or otherwise, and no women we spoke to found themselves drawn to the high jinks of Chippendales.

While some of you may breathe easier with this news, we think that the idea of taking a day to celebrate friendship, at the time in your life you are about to commit to focus your attention and your loyalty on one person, is a good and balanced opportunity to remind yourself and others that friends will always be treasured and important to you. If the traditional lewd parties make little sense, there is still an opportunity here for a celebration that has a kind of lovely logic to it.

Let me begin by telling you right out that my views are, apparently, anachronistic about gender. Science is, this year, on the side of difference. Men and women are, so they say, not made the same way, but I don't buy it. There is so much evidence to support each side that one can't get a toe hold

in a squabble, but when the science card is pulled, all the emotional, in-the-gut arguments seem to fly out the window. I can tell you that the generation reaching maturity now seems to exhibit fewer gender behavior differences than their older brothers or sisters or that of their parents. They've been raised in an atmosphere with a fairer hand. They don't remember a time when women couldn't go or be or learn or try just about anything. "Free to Be You and Me" seems to have paid off. And if the playing field isn't level yet, it is better than it's been in most of recorded history.

Still, the stereotypes roll on. Men, we hear, won't use time together to talk about their fears or their joys. They may joke about them, and in the laughter, we may hear their anxieties. But if their willingness to talk and share their emotions may not happen when the men of a wedding party take off together for dinner or a basketball game, their presence in one another's lives at such a time must be noted and comforting. At the very least, it's distracting from the tensions and stress of family, budgets, planning and all of the hoopla that happens around a wedding.

Women, on the other hand, seem to thrive on connection. As long as there have been societies, I suspect, women have supported one another through births and deaths, delights and tragedies,

send-offs and homecomings. The truth is, they've draped the doors for funerals, they've stitched the banners for parades and they've talked one another through the best and the worst of life. Here is the open acknowledgment of emotional response that holds a culture together. No matter whom you love and marry, your women friends are part of your spine and you are part of theirs.

This celebration of friendship can be one of so many things. My favorite idea is to learn something new together. Dixie Todd, the New England party organizer, tells of a bride who took her bridesmaids to a famous chocolatier to learn how to make chocolate truffles. I know of a well-known New York florist who will give private lessons in flower arranging. Chef Mario Batali's high end wine store, Italian Wine Merchants, will create a tasting of Italian wines with antipasti and a host to guide you through the varieties and producers. If your town doesn't seem to offer these kinds of things, just ask. We suspect that you could arrange within twenty miles of most good-sized townships private lessons for everything from sushi and cake decorating to car repair, decoupage, water ballet or tightrope walking. Think of it as an adventure and call it what you will. As for the New American Bridegroom, he—and his—can—and probably will—play golf.

All my reports back tell me that the old, traditions of Rehearsal Dinners or Grooms Dinners seem to have been replaced by the prewedding guest gathering made essential by our mobility. As weddings call us back to our friends from far-flung points, accommodations are now made for the Wedding Weekend rather than simply the Wedding Day. It seems that the most likely scenario accounts for a get-together on Friday evening with the wedding on Saturday, running into the night, and a brunch on Sunday before everyone heads back to whatever coast, land, island or borough they've traveled from. The party planners to whom I spoke seemed to concur that for more "planned" weddings, the idea of

contrast is likely to be exercised at this Friday event. So, if the wedding is a picnic, the Friday dinner is likely to be sit-down and more formal. If the wedding is dressy and done, the Friday dinner will be informal.

Susan Bednar and John Long created an experience for their guests in Italy that included a trip to Torcello by motor launch and an outdoor garden dinner, where everyone was asked to dress like a star on the Italian Riviera. The guests ran away with the concept. Here we see sunglasses, Gucci, Pucci and awning stripes, strappy sandals and big tawny hair, gutsy costume jewelry and narrow Capri pants. Where do you think Capri pants came from, anyway?

Susan Bednar and John Long's prewedding

Italian Riviera party in Torcello

Sara Hudson and Ron Gold bring up a very sensitive issue—that of cost. Back in the days when parents paid for these things, the rehearsal dinner was picked up by the groom's parents. But when couples (in their twenties or fifties) are paying for the events themselves, their parents' tabs are no longer to be counted on.

If you are managing the ceremony and the reception in ways that attempt graciously to accommodate groups of people and deliver an entertaining, moving and meaningful experience, you must expect that the cost is going to be considerable. Feeding a large group of people, however simply, is an expense most of us can't take for granted. Add to this the venue, the decor, the dresses, the invitations, all the things this book is about—and you have a hefty little price tag to budget and manage.

Sara reminds us that the one thing she and Ron didn't account for was the fact that so many of their friends would choose to arrive the day before the wedding and stay until the day after. They'd never allowed for the expense

of feeding them two more meals, and it created a more than reasonable dose of angst just prior to their wedding.

There are a number of ways this can be addressed. One of the most gracious would be to let a good friend make the calls and organize a shared dinner, where the guests might divide the check and pick up the tab for the wedding hosts on the Friday-night dinner. Another is the gracious, careful and very delicate way Sara and Ron wrote to each guest, informing them of the fact that many of them were choosing to arrive on Friday and suggesting that they might individually call the inn to confirm their arrival and their reservations for dinner. Additionally, if you can arrange it, an announcement via note or e-mail might let guests know that the restaurant or inn has created a special prix fixe for the prewedding meal or postwedding brunch. With this, you might be seen as the messenger of good news, rather than the bearer of the fact that you are not actually paying for these meals.

Conversely, you can, as Susan and John did

for their Italian wedding, consider the whole weekend as one big event and budget accordingly. In our case, all three meals took place on our property—the Friday dinner on our stone terrace, under a clear, star-lit sky; the wedding, as noted, in the field, on the porch and in the tent on a warm and lovely September day; and the Sunday brunch—with more than a gaggle of us, gathered in the tent on a morning as rainy, dark and muddy as one's imagination could create. But it became the scene of a great jam session as my brothers, both brilliant musicians, with me tagging along on piano, and any number of Bloody Mary–primed guests playing and singing

blues and folk, Rogers and Hart, Randy Newman and Sondheim, songs our parents danced to, songs our grandparents taught us, through second helpings of scrambled eggs, corn-bread French toast, country ham and biscuits.

The mood was elated, the tension gone. The obvious delight in our wedding's having so narrowly missed bad weather created an atmosphere of relief and good cheer that was almost the best part of the wedding weekend for me. But it was the ragtag band and the slightly disheveled nature of all, bride and groom included, that I loved most. Not for everyone, I know. That's the point.

CHAPTER 5

BRIDAL REGISTRY

TOASTERS AND FONDUE SETS, CHAMPAGNE FLUTES, WAFFLE MAKERS, AND ALL MANNER OF VASES AND BOWLS, PLATTERS AND PLATES: THE STUFF THAT BRIDAL REGISTRIES ARE MADE OF.

Commemorative gifts are what the industry calls presents given for weddings, anniversaries, Mother's Day, Father's Day and the occasions of big celebrations, like the opening of a new home or the announcement of a big promotion or award. We know a lot of things about these gifts. We know that most commemorative gifts tally up at the cash register between $100 and $450. We know that in almost every modern society the price tag of a commemorative gift is culturally set. In other words, regardless of whether you are a manicurist or a movie mogul, if you spend less than $100 or more than $500, you look as though you don't understand the Rules. Intimate friends and family don't count. There, you can do what you like—give a condo in Vail or a jar of home-made tomato sauce, the point is, your personal connection with the one being gifted allows you to indulge them in ways that outsiders may or may not understand.

If you're playing by the rules, perfect commemorative gifts have status labels and neutral style. There are two reasons for this: we often give gifts to those whose homes we've not visited, and we hope the gift will be used and treasured far into the future. Fashions, we know, have a way of changing, so too much style is worrisome. A tony label is a kind of insurance that suggests the brand may be understood or appreciated, even if the gift is not. For example, a classic vase in a Tiffany box says it all. In fact, a new bride wrote my mother a thank-you note years ago apologizing for not writing sooner, with the excuse that she couldn't bring herself to open the present—such was the iconic power of the Tiffany box.

But what do you do about registering when the fact of joining forces with someone you love gives you two households full of waffle makers and platters, toasters and fondue sets? What do you do if you set up house with your partner years ago and are just now getting around to making it legal? What do you do if the things you treasure are not material things? What do you do if you love material things but are so darned picky that you'd never trust anyone to give you just what you want, just the way you want it?

Bridal registries are big business and the act of registering is something akin to taking the bar exam. You are given forms and facts and it takes days and days to fill them out and make your choices. Twenty years ago and more, this process was undertaken by a girl and her mother; the system was almost entirely manned and attended by women. For the last fifteen years attendance has been almost entirely shared by both the bride and the groom. Those of us in marketing think we can set the date that ended the importance of fine, bone, flowered china by the week that men, as if on cue, took over the role of the mother at the counter in the bridal registry. And the changes were greater than "solid" over "patterned" china. These changes grew into the following: bridal registries at Home Depot and Sears Tool Department; the casual nature of entertaining and dining; the removal of the wall between the kitchen and the dining room; the

proliferation of menswear colors into home design; the restaurant stove, the Jenn-Air indoor grill, the kitchen equipment that looks as though it might belong in a garage or a factory. This is not your mother's Harvest Gold appliance; this is the front of a Hummer.

And while it may not yet be the norm, these hardware and eclectic brands are eating into the registry departments of specialty and department stores, which created entire floors around the process of taking a bride from the fine silver to the crystal and then over to the china; then trotting her down to the housewares department and up the escalator to choose bedding and towels. Exhausting. Can you bring the tablecloths to the china department?

Not so easily. Single focus catalogs and stores, like Williams Sonoma, do a big business in registry with smart, easy forms and good coordination to their websites and their brick and mor-

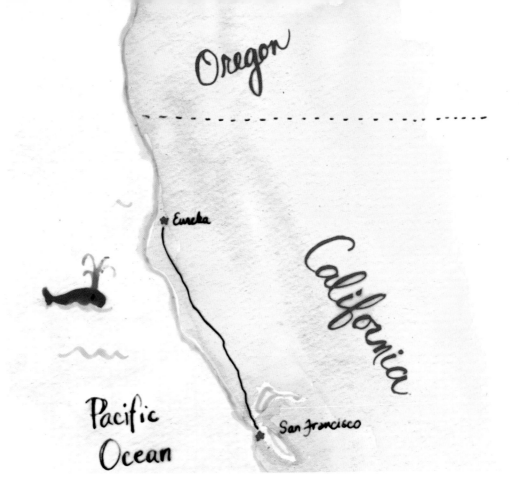

tar shops. Older couples (givers and giftees) still want to see things in person.

The younger couples we interviewed, however, had no problem with the idea of registering online. A few had chosen the cyber method over the idea of visiting stores because it fit their schedules and allowed them to keep track of their bounty. Even more of our couples had interests in gifts that were not material. Sometimes the two combined—the nonmaterial with the web focused, that is. Here's one: Sarah Morris and Jeff Michael found a website called the Big Day Honeymoon Registry that allowed

them to plan a road trip up the West Coast. Their friends and family can buy into this trip with hotel stays, meals, massages, special sights or events and even a movie. The options are managed in doses that allow someone to purchase and give a portion of an expensive stay or take on the whole toll. Sarah reported that she was nervous to bring the web concept to the more traditional of her family, but many have seemed to endorse the idea of creating memories and have loved the way it has allowed them to share in the planning of the trip.

Another trend we found was the request for good deeds. Cathy Guisewite, the creator of the comic strip "Cathy," works as a volunteer to a pet rescue organization in Southern California. Her new husband, Irv, joined her in asking for donations to Pet Orphans of Southern California, in lieu of gifts. *The New York Times'* "Vows" column featured a couple who married at Christmas and collected as their gifts Toys for Tots, a charity that gets a lot of play on the media during New York's holiday broadcasts. The bride admitted that she had to keep the groom from playing with too many of the toys.

Nic York and Matt Bogen did some research to find that in their Los Angeles area, there is no shortage of clothes for the needy, but there is a real need for underwear. It makes sense, doesn't it?, we think to donate a sweater or a coat that may no longer be the height of fashion but still warm and serviceable, and yet most of us would not dream of passing on our old drawers. The slightly wacky idea of underwear gifts melded with the practical, and Nic and Matt collected hundreds of sets of new underwear for both men and women to donate to shelters in their home town.

I've always thought the idea of "collections" might be a great way to register. I have a friend

whose collection of antique maps gives many of us a chance to indulge him while learning more about a new subject, investing more of our spirit in "the hunt," allowing us to enjoy, just a tad more, the whole process of giving. Maybe the two of you could find something you both love—old cameras, ironstone pitchers, wooden boxes, vintage linens, midcentury glass or turn-of-the-last-century letter openers. Focusing the pack on choices more personal and individual than housewares or towels could make it far more fun for all.

Many of the invitations we looked at contained notes in tiny mouse-size type, like that of Joyce Castleberry and Gerry Hovagimyan: "Your presence, no presents." Or Anne Watkins and David Millman's invitation that read, "Your presence is gift enough." In every case, however, whether the no-gift rule was enacted or not, gifts were given. Most of them were and are loved, and that's the good news there. But don't assume that a statement on your invitation saying "no gifts" will spare you the seven salad sets. Family and friends want to be a part of the good-will surrounding joy, and they can't be expected to comprehend your closets' overflowing with material proof of your past. My advice: give them something to do.

Frank and I fell deep into the too-much-stuff category and were about to put the tiny mouse-typed note on our invitations as well, when a friend took me aside and gave me advice. No one, she said, will pay any attention. She was clear in her opinion that the people who follow the no-gift rule will worry that they should have done something anyway and they'll have anxiety. More, she assured me, will just ignore the note and buy us something we don't want.

As a child, one of my favorite birthday presents had been a dogwood tree, planted by my father, outside my bedroom window at my parents' house in the country. It was on their property, of course, but we all thought of it as "my" dogwood tree. The year my father died, the tree died—supporting the whole idea of how interconnected all living things might be.

Frank and I twisted and turned for a while about the registry thing, and then I remem-

bered the dogwood story. Our house was called DogWood Farm, and it all fell into place. We decided to register at our local nursery, where a rose bush might be purchased for well under fifty dollars. The idea seemed to capture the imaginations of our friends and we were showered with roses and lilies and lilacs and, yes, dogwoods. Our friends' good wishes for us will bloom and grow each year and we'll tend them with extra care.

Like everything else in this book, we believe that each choice you make says something about you. Don't for a minute feel that you need to follow anyone else's agenda on the registry front. In this, like all else, listen to your own good sense. With everything available and acceptable, from travel to charity, towels to antique books, pear trees to potato peelers and, of course, the classic vase from Tiffany, you're sure to make the right choice.

CHAPTER 6

THE DRESS

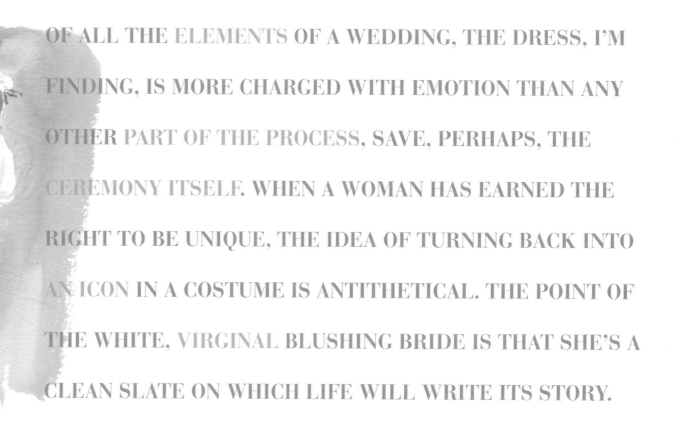

OF ALL THE ELEMENTS OF A WEDDING, THE DRESS, I'M FINDING, IS MORE CHARGED WITH EMOTION THAN ANY OTHER PART OF THE PROCESS, SAVE, PERHAPS, THE CEREMONY ITSELF. WHEN A WOMAN HAS EARNED THE RIGHT TO BE UNIQUE, THE IDEA OF TURNING BACK INTO AN ICON IN A COSTUME IS ANTITHETICAL. THE POINT OF THE WHITE, VIRGINAL BLUSHING BRIDE IS THAT SHE'S A CLEAN SLATE ON WHICH LIFE WILL WRITE ITS STORY.

When Frank and I set the date for our wedding, the theme and the details fell into place with ease. An American country fair concept allowed us to be at our own home in the country with our friends and family—children, dogs, gardens, games and great American food. I had help from some very talented people, but I think they'd agree that we set the tone and the tasks pretty quickly for all things creative and celebratory. Everything, that is, except The Dress.

The Dress: this is the part where I play "The Bride," I thought; this is the "bride's costume." But the more I tried to imagine myself in a white bridal dress, the more like a costume it seemed and though I searched the pages of brides' magazines and bridal books and reviewed what must have been a thousand dresses, I could find no reference that hit a mark for me or spoke to my kind of style. I understood the bride fantasy thing, but for me, real life felt better than fantasy —or at least any fantasy I'd conjured. Was I the only one who felt this way? Clearly not.

I had been to weddings of friends who didn't want to look like princess brides or Halloween floats. They appeared to solve the problem by wearing to their ceremonies what my mother would have christened "a very nice suit." It might have had a designer label and my pals might have looked lovely, but they rarely looked different from, or better than, their guests. I didn't want that, either.

My best friend, Amy, took her bridesmaid duties to heart. She was frustrated when I procrastinated and, perhaps, justifiably annoyed when the best I could come up with was the promise to wear a clean blouse with my jeans. "You have to deal with this," she kept saying. "The wedding is in three months—eight weeks—three weeks! You're the bride! You have an obligation here!"

Two weeks before the wedding, I solved my problem like Scarlett O'Hara, with yards and yards of silk drapery taffeta in two scales of gingham. While Amy's dressmaker sewed up my ad hoc version of a bride outfit, no book had put it

this page:

illustration of silk

gingham of my taffeta

wedding stole

opposite page:

Zoran's transparent,

gazar anorak

this page:

me on my

wedding day

opposite page:

Maggie Norris for

Ulla Maija, an equestrian-

inspired wedding outfit

together for me. No magazine had pointed the way and I knew that my circumstances had to be reproduced thousands of times all across America. There had to be countless brides who didn't fit the mold and didn't want to, but certainly felt no less delighted, no less loved, no less worthy of celebration.

So often the personal issues of my own life have reflected the societal changes I've noted for clients, and this time proved no exception. I could feel the ground moving under my feet, even as I searched for a way to present myself in the ceremony of my life. And if, in time, I found my own way and my own style, as soon as the wedding was over I made it my business to pick up the hunt of what I thought was a great example of social change: the transformation of ritual in its reflection of the culture. And for me, it all started with the idea of The Dress.

Personalization was affecting every aspect of our lives from iPods to Mini-Coopers. How was it possible The Dress had not succumbed? Finally, after months of review I can finally report that there is no doubt about it, a significant newcomer has arrived on the horizon: a bride who doesn't look like a meringue; a bride who doesn't necessarily look like The Bride. This is not about age; for example, neither Kate Hudson nor Liv Tyler married in traditional wedding dresses.

Maggie Norris, the Bergdorf Goodman couturier, sees the highest end of retail and offers wonderful possibilities. One resembles a dressage-riding habit, including a top hat, bustle and very fitted and boned-silk hacking jacket. It is original, fresh, quirky, personal—all the things a New American Bride's apparel might require to fit the personality of a stylish, grown-up woman who is still a little horse crazy.

I wondered whether there was a new customer for bridal or was the original customer changing before our eyes? First of all, Maggie agreed, these hints to new behavior were in-

deed real, and the styles they suggest might be basic and practical, almost sportswear in their assembly, or pure fantasy—but if it's New American Wedding thinking, it's fantasy based on fact—the notes of a woman's own life and they add up to unusual, and very personal, choices for women who have earned the right to see themselves as unique.

In other words, the embodiment of the trend is a bridal outfit (dress or otherwise) that breaks the rules and celebrates the individual rather than the concept of a bride. Once more I was reminded, It's not your mother's wedding.

Maggie Norris is known for hauntingly beautiful, made-to-order eveningwear dresses with corsets that can require as many as fifty measurements from the couture departments of Bergdorf Goodman and Neiman Marcus. She works with Charles Bunstine, who is also the owner of Ulla Maija, Bergdorf and Neiman's leading wedding gown resource.

"Yes, there is definitely a new bride on the scene," they confirm. More and more, the brides who make their way to Maggie and Charles hope to look like themselves, to express something of their own style, and not slavishly adopt a traditional bridal look.

"We ask them about the clothes they wear in real life, the clothes that make them comfortable," Maggie explains. "We talk about their lifestyle and the choices they've made in how and where they live. Then we talk about how the wedding reflects the rest of their lives." The bridal couturier as shrink? "There have been times," Maggie and Charles say, "when we've been desperate enough for direction, that we've asked a customer the following question: If this wedding were a movie, what would the movie be called and who'd be playing you?"

It's a shrewd question that somehow leads Charles and Maggie on a direct through line to distinct types like Jean Arthur versus Jean Harlow, and I worry about the five-foot-eight-inch size sixteen who smoothes back her mud-brown hair and suggests that Nicole Kidman would be perfect for the role. But this, I guess, is just part of

their genius, because the dresses in the collections of Maggie Norris and Ulla Maija undeniably evoke all manner of personal styles.

"Of course, there is still the young-girl bride, brought to us by her mother, and no matter how lovely she might look in a dress, until the mother sees the dress she wants, there's no sale. These can be wonderful, touching moments—and we're delighted to be part of them—but there is no question in my mind that this new bride you're talking about is beginning to seriously influence our market."

Charles chipped: "There's definitely a change in the business. And it's not just about the dress," he asserted. "It's about the couple. I was a New American Groom!" and he proceeded to tell me about his own wedding and his involvement in it. His wife was dressed like no bride of no century past, in a lustrous satin coat dress, made just for her by Carolyn Roehm; a dress as modern and yet as classic as could be. Most of all, it was a dress that showed off, to best advantage, her sassy, modern style, her cap of auburn hair and her very beautiful legs. Not a point lost on Charles. He used it as a great bit of direction.

"Dress the woman," he said, "the real woman. Make the best of her best qualities and be aware that something very flattering and very personal is likely to withstand the terrors of time."

While dresses by Carolyn Roehm, Maggie Norris and Ulla Maija may not be in everyone's budget, they are, nonetheless, directional and they show us the way to think about the choices we make. Budgets aren't really the deciding factor here. It's creativity and fresh thinking, not money, that will meet the challenge of creating a new style for brides. And against all odds, there are women, young, old and in between, creating a new style, with very little outside direction. All of us, no matter what our means, are simply following the compass inside our heads and hearts.

Here are some examples:

Debbie Bain found her white linen spaghetti-strap summer sun dress on the rack at Brooks Brothers. No frills, no trains, no beading, no big price tag. Could there have been a dress more perfect for a midsummer family wedding in a warm church?

Artist Anne Watkins knew she and her soon-to-be-husband, David Millman, would be married in a small ceremony at home. They wanted all the intimacy being at home suggested. The decision was simple; dressing for the event was not. Anne and a friend set out on The Dress hunt with all of New York to explore. After days of searching and rejecting dress after dress, Anne's friend turned to her and asked why none of the pretty things they'd seen could be made to work. "I'd never wear that at home" was Anne's answer.

"Okay. What do you wear at home?" asked her friend, swimming toward the only raft she saw in the rough sea of wedding dresses.

"Pajamas," Anne replied immediately.

A trip to Frette uncovered red cashmere pajamas. And that was Anne's very appropriate and very comfortable answer to her struggle with The Dress.

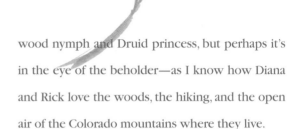

Diana McSpadden knew she wanted a nontraditional wedding dress for her mountaintop Vail, Colorado, celebration. To be more accurate, just like most of us, she knew even better what she didn't want. And for months she kept her eyes open for just the right dress. On a vacation in Hawaii, she came across a dressmaker who'd crafted gowns of gossamer beauty, no two alike. They had the hand of the artist about them with an almost impossible suggestion of nature mixed with whimsy. Diana and the dressmaker corresponded; muslin samples were created and shipped between Colorado and Hawaii. She had to find a local dressmaker to manage the fitting of the muslin and send it back and forth, hoping the pins and the notes would suffice to decipher. There were moments when Diana wondered what she'd gotten herself into, counting on a dress's being sewn more than half a continent away. She questioned whether or not it would, indeed, really be all right in the end. It was. The dress proved everything she hoped it would be.

To me, Diana's dress is somewhere between wood nymph and Druid princess, but perhaps it's in the eye of the beholder—as I know how Diana and Rick love the woods, the hiking, and the open air of the Colorado mountains where they live.

This happy story with a good end misses a crucial point: Why was finding The Dress made so difficult? Diana McSpadden found the right dress, but she found it halfway around the world. The tough part is this, while we're listening to our own drummers, we're not seeing the dresses that dance to the music.

this page:

the groom sees

the bride dressed

for their wedding

opposite page:

Diana McSpadden's and

Rick Todd's wedding

clothes await them

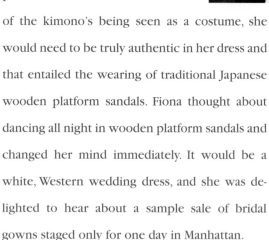

Fiona Gallahue tells a chilling story about visiting the sample sale of a famous bridal designer. In balancing the Celtic Western and traditional Japanese influences of her wedding, she'd seriously considered wearing a wedding kimono. Her future mother-in-law, however, pointed out that to avoid the effect of the kimono's being seen as a costume, she would need to be truly authentic in her dress and that entailed the wearing of traditional Japanese wooden platform sandals. Fiona thought about dancing all night in wooden platform sandals and changed her mind immediately. It would be a white, Western wedding dress, and she was delighted to hear about a sample sale of bridal gowns staged only for one day in Manhattan.

Fiona is a trauma doctor with not much time to spare and yet she managed to be in line just after the advertised opening of the doors. "Not too bad," she thought of the line she could see. Beyond the doors, however, waited a much longer

line of girls who had arrived even earlier. Waiting time seemed interminable, but finally Fiona got inside. The sight of the dresses beyond the frenzied girls was almost frightening. Out of their size racks and raked across aisles, the dresses were twisted and stretched, with girls hissing at one another like women in a rerun of *I Love Lucy*. When Fiona spotted a sign that listed SALE-BEHAVIOR-DON'TS and included an instruction for NO BITING, she left, determined that the Brooklyn emergency room of her work was a far safer place.

Fiona's dress saga also had a happy ending when she found a resource that sells wedding gowns donated from the finest manufacturers and turns the profits over to children's charities. Her dress, simple and elegant, nodded to tradition in a ceremony that meant to respect more than one.

In marketing, we have a creed when it comes to establishing a brand's identity against

this page:

Fiona Gallahue

and Retsu Takahashi

at their wedding

opposite page, top:

Nic York plays The Bride

in her costumed wedding

bottom: Nic and

Matt Bogen, her groom

its competition: You can beat them by staking a different claim, or you can join them; but if you join them—you have to beat them at their own game. Much of what we explore in this chapter encourages brides to find their own voice and their own style in how they choose to present themselves at their wedding. We urge them not to wear what would amount to a costume.

We have one brilliant example of the opposite approach: Nic York was to be married to Matt Bogen in Los Angeles. Somehow along the

way, looking at bridal books, trying on gowns, it occurred to her that The Bride outfit was exactly that which had occurred to me—a costume. And she decided to take the challenge head on and make it the most wonderful costume at a costume ball.

Her attendants wore costumes, too: Renaissance and empire dresses; one wore wings, many wore masks. A good time was had by all and Nic looked the part of the very beautiful bride from the tip of her over-the-top tiara to the sole of her white silk shoe.

this page:

for Chado-Ralph Rucci,

a white wool crepe dress

with twig embroidery

opposite page:

Rucci's white ottoman

and translucent

sheer dress with bright

feather-filled skirt

In the dozens of weddings I've attended, the bride always looked like a bride. Ten days after the event I could not tell you what her dress looked like. Was this because she wasn't, after all, representing herself but playing a bride in a bride costume? Ralph Rucci echoes this idea: "I don't make wedding gowns," he said.

"No?" I ask, surrounded by some of the most spectacular dresses on the market, all unique and wonderful.

"Not wedding dresses," I hear him say, and yet many of these dresses are special in just the ways I imagine could break the mold of our expectations.

For a daytime wedding in a judge's chambers, a short white crepe dress, embroidered with winter white twigs and inset with bits of gazar is tailored and unorthodox. This could, after all, be a wedding outfit that might defy and elevate the most somber and corporate of environments.

With style, detail and the light touch of ge-

nius transcending both the silhouette and even the intent of the "tailored dress," this completely nontraditional choice is one of the best examples of New Thinking for bridal dressing that I can imagine. But Ralph has a number of other wonderful options.

His short dress, of white ottoman with sheer gazar neck and shoulders, is a crisp and strict little dress until you get to the hemline, filled and aflutter with poison green feathers. Perfect for a woman who seems all business and discipline,

but who possesses the most delightful, and even sexy, streak of wit.

Ralph Rucci's sheer nude embroidered bodice, paired with a taupe gazar skirt and wrap are also bold fashion choices and only for his couture customers. But this outfit points to an important direction—that romance can be had within a discipline that approaches sportswear and an ease that suggests more about the woman who wears the clothes than the clothes that wear the woman.

this page: Rucci's white chiffon

ruffled short dress

his sheer-embroidered

top with mocha gazar

skirt and shrug

opposite page:

luminosity creates drama—

Ralph Rucci suit and stole

In the same vein is his white pleated chiffon dress that appears as innocent and easy as could be, but carries a level of detail and sophistication that could not come inexpensively or without determined thought.

A spectacular evening coat in coffee duchess satin over a pearl-beaded top may be another choice for a woman of substance who wants to wear something long but still loves the idea of cutting a familiar sportswear figure.

For women who may not (or may no longer) have the figures of willowy models, Ralph Rucci creates silhouettes that transcend perfect bodies. His tunics glide smoothly over pants and his embroidered caftans create drama, beauty, clean lines and attention to detail while keeping secrets.

If couture can be afforded, this could be the answer to so many issues we harbor. The shape may be dramatic but it always answers to a strict and controlled discipline of line and scale.

this page:

duchess satin evening coat

and beaded top

suggest a sophisticated

separates approach to

wedding dressing

opposite page:

Chado-Ralph Rucci's sheer

caftan in white

The showstopper of one Rucci fashion show was a dress that brought an audience of jaded fashionistas to their feet. Named the "Infanta," it is a little more typical of what a bride who wants to be "white and center" might choose, yet it defies any suggestion of a typical gown. Ralph gives us, once again, though this time in spades, the unexpected and unparalleled mix of froth and architecture, like foam on a wave, reinforcing what so many believe—that in the world of fashion, Ralph Rucci is America's living treasure. Some think the world hasn't seen his like since Balenciaga cut his own cloth; I am in this camp. But perhaps because he is so private, what few know is what a civilized and gentle man he is; generous, thoughtful, level and kind. And while we often find examples of the opposite, it does make you reflect on how often the worth of the art is parallel to the worth of the man who created it.

this and opposite pages:

Rucci's Infanta. A showstopper

of a dress combines

flourishes and

architectural discipline

I

In another exercise of control and creativity, Susan Bednar married John Long in Venice wearing a dress she designed in collaboration with Danielle Gisiger of Ateliers Danielle Gisiger, NYC. Susan, you see, loves aquamarine and after rejecting the idea of wearing a dress of aqua or turquoise, she backed into the idea of the aquamarine bustle. Her dress is duchess satin and an interesting mix of old and new influences; just, she tells me, like the environments she creates as an interior designer. She accessorized with an aquamarine tulle veil, Bruno Magli aqua and silver shoes and, of course, jewelry set with her beloved aquamarines.

this and opposite pages:

Susan Bednar's duchess satin dress

with aqua bustle and veil

On a much different scale, at my own wedding, I wore my huge taffeta gingham stole with a coordinating but smaller scale gingham taffeta, made up to copy one of my Zoran tops. I paired them with pale taupe silk pants, also by Zoran, and much worn over the years with everything from a gazar anorak to a cashmere sweater, from the theater to black-tie dinners.

But Zoran's clothes are like that. His shapes are his "signature shapes"—forgiving and gentle—and his fabrics are solid color, luxurious but simple. No wonder he's been the choice for many brides looking for an unorthodox choice. Women look like themselves in his clothes, no matter how elegant the fabrics. His charmeuse T-shirts and soft jackets continue to express a personally confident, casual chic.

The New Yorker magazine's Joyce Castleberry wore a long white silk dress with Zoran's white duchess satin jacket to her own country church wedding. She looked fantastic; and while as beautiful as any bride, she also managed to look just like the Joyce I know so well—tailored, classic and pretty as can be.

There is no doubt that for so many women, The Dress is far more than a dress. It stands for things we wish we always were and things we're proud to be. If it can make us feel taller or thinner or more confident, all the better. If it can wipe out some of the harshness that life has tossed our way, better still.

Some years after Sara Hudson divorced, she found herself in a dressmaker's shop in the East Eighties of Manhattan. There in front of her was a dress; not a wedding dress, but a kind of confection of tiered, ruffled and yet understated and restrained lace. It wasn't white, but its subtle, mellowed tea-stained elegance suggested, she thought, the idea that romance might still exist in a life that had seen its share of truths. She asked the price and paled; the cost was far more than she could

part with while raising a daughter as a single parent. But she came back to the shop and to the dress that called to her. The dressmaker listened to her story, fitted the dress to her still Ford Model figure, and allowed Sara to pay in increments over a year. At last the dress was hers; the dress she knew she would wear at her Next Wedding.

Years went by, her daughter grew up. Sara dated and didn't date, and finally fell in love. And nearly twenty years after wrapping the dress in tissue and putting it on a high shelf in her closet, she climbed up her stepladder and took down the dress once more. There is yet another happy ending to this story in that the dress was every bit as wonderful as Sara remembered; the perfect combination of hope and grace. After all these years, I wondered, how did it fit? Sara laughed and told me that indeed, it had been a little tight; but a combination of diet and alterations took care of that.

And so Sara Hudson wore it on her Hudson River wedding day, carrying with her the idea of all the years she'd spent not quite forgetting what was waiting for her on the top shelf.

Clare Henry knew that her whole wedding would be about art. Clare writes from New York on art for London's *Financial Times*. Her husband, Phillip Bruno, runs one of America's most prestigious galleries. For a wedding in a chapel conceived in art to a reception in an artist's loft, what might she wear that would speak the language of art without being a costume?

Clare spotted the fabric of her dress on what the Scots call "the peg"; in other words, a store-bought dress, rather than one made for her. Or was it? The full taffeta skirt of the dress was graphic with artist palette colors. The skirt might have delighted her, but the strapless black bodice read both dark and bare. Even more problematic,

and less flattering, she explained, was the full cummerbund-sashed waist.

If art has a place in the challenge, however, count on Clare to take up the cause. She bought the dress, problems and all. Because she is so fond of Mother of Invention solutions, she took her scissors to the sash the moment she got it home. The offending thick cummerbund was purged. The sash became a stole to wrap around her shoulders, and the dress was no longer all black or all bare on top. A brilliant and artistic solution materialized for a woman with no fear of taking arts and crafts into her own hands.

How many brides wind up dancing in their bare feet? Far too many it seems. For all the Jimmy Choos and the Manolos that make our hearts beat faster, there is a little taunting voice of practicality straining to be heard. How can you dance all night in shoes you've not broken in? And how can you dance all night in five-inch heels and a toe box that would be too narrow for a Doctor Seuss Grinch?

If you're mature enough to resist the temptation to believe that your toes are really long and pointy, there exists an alternative so smart you may wonder why no one has ever offered it before. Broadway dancer Phil LaDuca spent nearly all his life in dance shoes. But dancers' careers are short; their heels and toes go and the years of hard landings after what appeared to be weightless leaps take their toll on dancers' backs. Some retire to teach, some to choreograph. Phil LaDuca moved on to create the world's most extraordinary dance shoes.

Phil discovered, if that word can be applied to an insight so basic that the addition of a higher toe box, a flexible sole and, most of all, his patented invention—an elastic gusset—allowed him to make character dance shoes that were as flexible as a ballet slipper but with superb support and balance. Until Phil, it seems no one had combined the looks costume designers craved with the padding and support dancers needed, and the extension choreographers only dreamed they'd see.

Phil's shoes, labeled "LaDuca," fit each foot perfectly because they are made, quite specifically, for each foot. And no two feet, says Phil, are the same—not even two feet on the same person.

this page:

LaDuca's handmade shoes as

backless mules are

passementerie trimmed

for a wedding

opposite page:

Susan Bednar

and John Long dance

at their wedding

At the most basic measurements, one foot is almost always a quarter to a half size larger and it's not unusual to find the difference even greater. Arches run higher or flatter, heels measure thinner or fatter, the distance between the ball of the foot and the heel may be of different proportions than the length of the right and left feet would suggest. It all adds up to the fact that we are walking around with square pegs in round holes every day. We may complain, we may limp, but dancers can shorten their careers if they incur one injury too many, dance in shoes that pinch or pitch their weight in the wrong direction.

Broadway dancers and theatrical costume designers have embraced Phil LaDuca and most of the singing and dancing shows now playing on Broadway tap to his beat—from the Witches' boots in *Wicked* to Bette Midler's Harlettes. In fact, if you've seen the movie *Chicago*, you've seen his shoes on Renée Zellweger, Richard Gere and Catherine Zeta-Jones.

One day, a Radio City Rockette was to be married, and the one thing she knew she wanted to do at her wedding was dance and dance and dance; call it a busman's holiday. Phil LaDuca was an early call in her planning and she asked for shoes pretty enough to walk down an aisle— strong and supportive, flexible and comfortable

enough to dance all night. Phil made her a pair of shoes in white satin with his famous gusset and a diagonal elasticized strap. She was just the first in a long line of dancers who have asked Phil to make shoes embellished with the lace from their wedding dresses or bits of embroidery, dyed silk, or silvered, or tied with satin bows.

He's also created shoes for just standing around looking wonderful, like lace frothed mules, and while they don't have the padding or the straps that might encourage you to dance all night, they are made to order, the left foot differs from the right. Most of all, they are your shoes. Made for you. Made to do what you want them to

do, look the way you want them to look, feel more comfortable than any shoes you've ever owned and, most of all, express the fact that only you might wear them.

If the idea of shoes fit for a dancer's feet but completely made to order for your own appeals to you, expect to pay in the neighborhood of what an exotic Jimmy Choo might cost and allow about six weeks from your fitting. But Phil says to tell you that he's turned on a dime for a client with a deadline. That his turns were still graceful seems certain.

top left:

Ellen Carrucci

and Will Tracy

at their Connecticut

shore-front wedding

top right:

Stephanie Wargo,

dressed for her wedding

bottom:

Ellen's Escada

shoes matched her outfit

When Ellen Carrucci married Will Tracy on their Connecticut beach, she wore her love of color brilliantly in a sweater and brocade paisley pants from Escada, the color of a Schiaparelli sherbet.

The part of her wedding outfit that most interested me? Ellen's shoes. Her elegant, rich pink mules were created from the same brocade fabric as her pants. These are the shoes of a woman who will never trip on a sidewalk or lose her balance coming down a flight of stairs. At work Ellen navigates the corridors of Condé Nast with style and confidence;

and the corridors of Condé Nast are not for the timid or the weak of heart. But is Ellen such a different animal from me?

On a cold winter's afternoon not long ago, I waited for a friend outside of the Condé Nast cafeteria. I closed my eyes to listen to the sound of fashion editors walking the hall. SLAP, SLAP, SLAP went their backless shoes against their bare heels, and with every tenth step or so came a stumble and a small swear word. SLAP, SLAP, SLAP, SLAP, stumble, swear, SLAP, SLAP, SLAP on down the hall. Impossibly tall, thin and self-possessed, these fashion girls rarely seem to

smile. Nothing, apparently, strikes them as quite good enough, which makes me want to strike them outright. Still, Ellen manages to work with and around them, keeping both her sense of style and her good humor intact. Many things make her smile. I look again at Ellen's wedding picture and note, with some relief, that a delighted Ellen is standing next to Will, looking as though life was quite good enough, thank you. And her feet, don't you just know it, are bare.

So there stands Ellen, on a rocky beach, barefoot in October and very much herself; which brings me to the point of self-expression in the spotlight. For many women who have run businesses or worked for large corporations, the idea of being in a spotlight is a nightmare worth an aria or two. We have managed to hold on to our sanity by doing two things: staying in control of what we do best and staying out of the spotlight. The whole process of being The Bride at a wedding will shake those two positions to the bone.

Like me, Stephanie Wargo put off thinking about what she would wear to her wedding; like

me, she thought that this technique of avoidance might actually work. But also like me, she had a helper hell-bent on intervention. Her sister stepped in and dictated the necessity for at least a new skirt and a new blouse.

Tailored, simple, minimal but not stark or cold, her outfit is as classic and graceful as Stephanie. She looks comfortable, pretty and, most of all, just like herself.

She did feel, however, that the outfit was a bit too delicate for the wearing of her signature silver necklace—a classically sportive piece that completely supports Stephanie's style. When she took the necklace off, she found that nature had stepped in to insist that she remain true to her own colors. There was a definite and stark tan line where her necklace sat, and she realized that she could not do without it. So, it might not have been bridal pearls or a delicate something borrowed, but in these pictures, you can see for yourself that the look couldn't have been more ideal.

For all the talk about bridal wear's reflecting a woman's personality, let me be clear. If there

are brides who want to be married in pajamas I endorse it. I applaud the Brooks Brothers sun dress as much as Ralph Rucci's Chado couture. The difference I'm finding between the New American Bride and her younger or less self-aware counterpart is usually a move toward the more refined, the more tailored, the more casual or the quieter side of fashion; apparel that lets the character of the woman rather than the personality of The Dress star in the event. But sometimes the bride's personality is big and self-assured and full of fun. How would a quiet dress support that kind of woman?

Zac Posen's sister Alexandra acts as his creative director. She deals with the practicalities of every such creative business—retailers, fashion editors, and problems in the factories. But she grew up in a happy home with an artistic and supportive mother and with Zac. Clearly their shared sense of creativity and fun go right back to the beginning of their lives and sparks both their relationship and their business.

This dress of "poppies, poppies, poppies" as Zac calls it, pays homage to their childhood, to Alex's beauty, to her whimsy and wit and to the gutsy sense of style Zac knows she has to pull off a bright red, tour de force of a wedding dress.

Alexandra and her artist groom, Nils Folke Anderson, were married in a field and wedding marched down a newly mowed aisle. The wedding was as stylish as could be. The day was perfect, the sky was blue, the field smelled of fresh-cut grass and the dress was more dress than anyone there had ever seen, but not too much dress for Alexandra. In fact, it was just right.

Zac defines it: "My clothing celebrates women and the expression of personality. My sister is a beautiful celebration of life, intelligence, creativity and fun. We've always shared a love for fantasy, perspective and theater. And—poppies, poppies, poppies, my dear…"

this page:

Alexandra Posen being laced

into her red-poppy wedding dress,

designed by her brother,

Zac Posen

following pages:

detail of the

poppy skirt and scenes

from the wedding

"AND—

POPPIES, POPPIES, POPPIES,

MY DEAR . . ."

ZAC POSEN

I sat in the ivory-tinted Ulla Maija showroom on a honey-colored velvet loveseat with peach and cream taffeta draping the windows, surrounded by dresses, none of them expected choices of frothy meringue and one more beautiful than the next, as Charles Bunstine, who was president of Barney's in its hottest fashion heyday, pointed out the extraordinary fact that there was not a single white dress in the room.

Suddenly all color was suggestion: all manner of creams—Devonshire to churned butter, soft white peach and early season apricot, baby's-cheek blush, tea with milk, mellow English china and Chinese blanc de chine, cameo, tea rose, latte, face powder and, most of all, pearl. "White—dead white," Charles advises, is rarely flattering. "It

this and following pages:
dresses from the
Ulla Maija Collection
speak to a sophisticated
bride who wants to
follow her own style

needs a hint of something more—fleshy, perhaps—to work with skin tones and create the synergy that lets the woman in the dress shine through."

His dresses, many designed by Maggie Norris, offer all manner of options that suggest fashion far more than something called a Wedding Gown. And if they are also white (or whatever shade of white we think we see), they have the power to express the personality and individuality of the woman who wears them.

But it isn't simply a matter of semantics—fashion versus style, gowns versus dresses, sportswear versus couture. There is something inherently modern in the idea of assuming a personal "look," rather than adapting to a code of dress that's imposed by the culture or a fashion magazine.

When I was growing up, there were prescribed fashion rules that apparently guarded the safety of our home as much as any other code of decent behavior, and I'm not just talking about the white-shoe-after-Labor Day ban. There were tennis whites and golf skirts, cocktail dresses and daytime dresses, business suits and evening gowns and never the twain would meet.

A lot of rules were enforced about what was appropriate. I remember my mother coming home from a luncheon (that's what they were called, "luncheons"—and until this very moment, nothing about this word struck me as odd) and announcing that Mrs. Van Nostrand wore a lovely dress, but it was not an "appropriate dress for a married woman." My great-grandmother nodded gravely, obviously understanding just what she meant; I still have no idea.

At eighteen I found my first little black dress at whatever followed the Bigi Boutique at Bergdorf Goodman. It was very *Breakfast at Tiffany's*. I planned to borrow my mother's pearls and wear it to Trader Vic's with a boy from Cornell but it went right back to Bergdorf's the next day. Completely inappropriate for someone my age, was the verdict. What was the saleswoman thinking? The whining that followed was met with the promise that we would talk about it again when I was twenty-one. By the time I was twenty-one all the rules had vanished.

But the rules about wedding dresses held on and on and on. Until now. If you, too, bridle at the

idea of bridal, know this: we are not alone. I feel strongly that the idea of separates and the way we dress in real life is beginning to take hold. In fact, J. Crew has added "Weddings" to its mix and offers a limited range of simple dresses that don't look very different from their standard party dresses; meaning, they have the same kind of sensibility and point of view. The clean-haired, headbanded, natural-nailed, long-legged, college-girl look that made it so successful is right here in its wedding section. No one from J. Crew is suggesting that for a wedding their customer should suddenly appear dressed as a cream puff or a boudoir pillow.

The chic options for weddings that Ralph Rucci and Zoran suggest may be created with opulent fabrics and handcrafted with skill and precision, beadwork or embroidery, dressmaker details far beyond what you might find in a workaday world. They take their cues from perfectly cut sportswear, coordinated separates, and from the lives of real women who know that to be truly stylish, one must be true to one's own nature.

NOTES ON "THE DRESS"

Now if you do want to waltz down the aisle like a princess-bride, far be it from me or anyone else to tell you otherwise. You'll have a lot of supporters with dozens upon dozens of bridal magazines; Amazon.com lists hundreds of books in the bridal category to help you decide between white and ivory, cream or ecru. There are helpful hints on choosing empire gowns, if you are short-waisted, or princess seams if your hips are full. At every price range you'll have all the help in the world. In the end, you'll look like a bride and though you will, no doubt, look beautiful, you might not necessarily be expressing the richest and rarest part of the wedding—you.

But if, like me, you've grown beyond that fantasy, and want to find something to wear that really showcases the essence of you and upholds the concept of the celebration you plan to express your life, here's the nut I think I've cracked; of these three rules pick one or pick all:

THREE WEDDING DRESS RULES

1
Dress like an actress in a movie about yourself

2
Dress for the theme of the event,
rather than the part of The Bride

3
Dress as though you're performing
in the same show as your guests, but dress
like the star, not a member of the chorus

Beyond these hints here are a few great rules collected from the masters we've talked to that you might remember, no matter where or how you solve the problem of what to wear when you are not an "iconic bride":

Luminosity

Whatever you wear should have some degree of luster. Silk and satin, charmeuse, gazar, taffeta, organza, organdy—choose fabrics that reflect light. More than any other aspect of the dress, stole or blouse, or any other garment you can imagine—short of a follow spot, nothing will do more to keep you in the spotlight at your wedding.

Timelessness

Be careful of following fashion at the expense of taste or a flattering cut. Remember—you will be looking at your wedding pictures decades from now and taste is not totally subjective. Time, you see, carries its own opinion. While a fashion statement might be having its moment, classic lines and a becoming cut will hold up over the years. Balance expressive style with an eye to the future.

Cross Cultures

Team a pair of silk pants with a rare, pale, Chinese silk kimono worn over a narrow tank top. It says ceremonial and dramatic but in a new, cultured and sophisticated way.

Signature Style

Try to find something that reflects your personality and your established sense of self. If you tend to sportswear and athletic clean lines, showing up in ruffles may not make sense. If you haven't been out of slacks since Walter Cronkite was in the newsroom, consider wearing soft cream cashmere pants and something like a silk charmeuse version of a sweater set.

Copy What You Love

Take your favorite article of clothing (something you know looks wonderful on you—a blouse or a jacket, a coat or a dress) and have it copied, note for note and line for line, in taffeta or satin, charmeuse or organza. You'll be comfortable and, most of all, you will look like you.

Finally, the point I endorse most in these new thoughts of how to dress for weddings and the pageants of our lives: making it "real" doesn't mean the absence of style. In a way, it defines the essence of true style; I suspect it's always been so.

CHAPTER 7

THE ATTENDANTS

ONCE UPON A TIME, I WAS IN A WEDDING AS ONE OF TWENTY BRIDESMAIDS. NO FLOUNCY DRESSES WERE IMPOSED ON US; INSTEAD, WE WERE INSTRUCTED TO WEAR SOMETHING PINK.

This didn't sound as painful as I'd dreaded though my wardrobe at the time was black. No one planned to force me into a tiered, ruffled, pleated, shiny dress. But pink?

As the "Art Director Bridesmaid," I was entrusted to pull all the bridesmaid looks together. The phone calls to my fellow maids suggested that I had my work cut out for me. I found disparate looks of all manner: a pale pink Chanel suit, a shocking pink satin ball gown, a coral pink sun dress, a striped linen caftan, a Lilly Pulitzer pink patterned skirt with T-shirt and, if you can imagine, everything in between. How could all this be quilted together, twenty times?

I tried to solve the coordinating issue with yards and yards of pale pink tulle and gave every-one some detail of the pink fluff to wear. In some cases it became a huge sash, in others it acted as a nest in the rim of a hat, or worked as a stole, or cuffs or a neck ruff. I know that it's hard to believe but it worked, and everyone seemed delighted. Most of all, it suggested ways in which freedom could win over the oppression of bridesmaid's-wear.

Our illustrator, Donna Mehalko, once designed a book called *101 Uses for a Bridesmaid's Dress*, which listed "floatation device" and "shower curtain" among the possible after-use options. Clearly, there was a market for this book. While it may be amusing, it shouldn't be this difficult.

When I was first married, in the seventies,

my bridesmaids were scattered in colleges across America. I designed bridesmaid dresses of heavy cream silk skirts and matching blouses with red velvet sashes. The dressmaker had only to learn their sizes to make the dresses, leaving just the hems to mark and stitch by hand, in the days before the wedding. And after the wedding, my friends had silk shirts to wear with their jeans and a long skirt to cut and hem to ballet or knee length.

opposite page:

Susan Bednar's

attendants in Jenny Yoo

striped dresses

groomsmen in Paul Stuart

seersucker suits

There has been some small movement away from all the matching pastel puffy bridesmaid dresses in the traditional bridal market. New options lean toward a coordinated approach to bridesmaid outfits, allowing attendants to choose tops and bottoms that might be more flattering to their figures, while still appearing to be playing in the same band. It may be a baby step, rather than a full sportswear approach, but it is a step in the right direction.

Susan Bednar wanted her theme of stripes to come across at every chance, and her bridesmaids' dresses, from Jenny Yoo, allowed her to do just that. Without looking like paper dolls, these fresh, fashionable striped dresses also came in styles that permitted each attendant to choose the shape that fit her taste and her figure best. Susan accessorized the looks with vintage Italian costume jewelry.

The groomsmen wore Paul Stuart's gray and cream seersucker suits and Ralph Lauren striped ties, again supporting the striped theme.

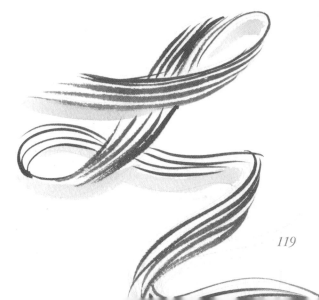

Sarah Morris and Jeffrey Michael knew enough about design to keep their wedding party to colors of gray and blue, as they planned to pose before the black and white images of an old movie. No bridal-department outfits were imposed on this wedding either, just flattering, pretty dresses that suited each girl. Neither was there hierarchy in the positioning; instead of bridesmaids, maid of honor, ushers and best man, Sarah and Jeff chose to call their attendants "Best Men" and "Best Women."

The Best Men wore gray suits, white shirts and cornflower blue ties. Sarah's twelve-year-old brother had broken his arm a few weeks before the wedding and requested a blue or gray cast so his arm wouldn't clash with the wedding colors.

Nic and Matt Bogen's wedding allowed each participant to engage in flights of fantasy. Nic saw this opportunity to "dress up" as a gift she could give each attendant. She encouraged and supported the amusement with accessories and a florist who would embrace the challenge of creative design, to the point where a bouquet became a flowered snake for Eve. Nic's favorite time of the wedding was the shared delight of transformation, as she and each of her attendants created looks born of whimsy, dreams and exhilarating flights of imagination.

Nic York wanted her attendants to create their own fantasies.

121

As Sara Hudson's dress had been ready and waiting for decades, her attention was taken up with finding something suitable for her daughter, Hadley. Looking at these pictures, one can't imagine a better choice for the location, the ceremony or the day than this soft, blue, sleeveless dress that supports rather than competes with the bride's dress. Sara's niece and nephew took center stage for more than a moment as they performed their walk down the aisle, preceding the bride. W. C. Fields did warn us to never appear onstage with a dog act or a child.

My discomfort with the spotlight must be real, as I made my entrance with not one dog in tow, but two. Technically, my bridesmaid was my dog, Coco. Her leash and collar were extravagantly laced with daisies and black-eyed susans to form a ruff and a bower, by the New York florist Zeze, in a sweep so brilliant that she got a full round of applause as she appeared on the porch. And Leonardo, the pug that belongs to my friend Amy and her husband, Steven Shapiro, appeared as the ring bearer, wearing a little gold and blue pillow on his back, also fashioned by Zeze, with our two rings tied in place.

But it was Amy who really took the job of attendant to heart. Dr. Amy Attas is a renowned

this page:

Coco, my maid of honor,

Amy Attas, my bridesmaid,

and Leonardo, the ring bearer,

with our treasures

tied to his back

New York City veterinarian, with a house-call practice that includes as clients the pets of the famous, the chic and the demanding. She works difficult hours and when she is not attending to a dog or cat in need, she is studying to learn more about every advance in her field. I wanted to honor her and my joy in our friendship, but I didn't expect that there would be much need for her to attend to me, as a bride. I was wrong.

I'd been so thrown by how little I'd seen in stores or magazines that seemed appropriate to our "farm" wedding that I found myself concentrating on everything but my appearance. I had a business to run, an event to plan and two homes to organize around a new partner; no wonder I was overwhelmed. But Amy pulled every creative trick she could think of to help me focus.

When I hadn't made an appointment to meet her dressmaker, she set out to prove to me just how clever he was by having him produce an outfit for her, just made for a barn dance—made, in fact, of old blue jeans. The swallow-tailed skirt, with its gingham insert and peplum gingham blouse, fit my stated concept of a theatrical approach to The Farm. She looked perfectly wonderful.

opposite page:

Sara Hudson and

daughter, Hadley,

remind us how important

it is to think of the scale

and style of the bride's

dress when choosing

a bridesmaid's dress

the littlest attendants

are still picture perfect,

even when they

are not "costumed"

NO RULES FOR THE ATTENDANTS

As someone who is not beyond suggesting pets as attendants, I would hardly list a
series of rules for you. Here, however, are some things to think about:

No book says you have to have any attendant.
If you feel that choosing any friend or relative over another could create tension,
go it alone. Plenty of brides we talked to did just that.

Don't be overly concerned about creating outfits that match.
The same dress rarely works well on two different girls with different coloring and
different figures. Think, instead, about creating a look—as Sara Morris did, in
choosing colors that supported her idea of a black and white film, or as in
Nic Bogen's idea of creating a scene of fantasy characters.

Give the men in your party a distinctive look.
We chose blue denim shirts, khaki pants, matching belts and matching Topsiders
for Frank's sons and my brothers and nephew. If you must go with a tux,
make their ties distinctive.

Given the rare occasions for most of us to dress in formalwear, it might be smart to allow a kind of "separates" approach to dressing. I love the whole idea of sportswear for formal dressing. There are so many more options in your own wedding look and that of your attendants' if you will just open your eyes to a larger idea of fashion, and not limit yourself to looks that seem predigested for bridal approval.

CHAPTER 8

THE CEREMONY

"WE ARE GATHERED TOGETHER

IN THE SIGHT OF GOD AND THESE

WITNESSES TO JOIN TOGETHER,

IN HOLY MATRIMONY,

THIS MAN AND THIS WOMAN . . ."

Most of us know nearly all the lines of this familiar ceremony by heart, even if we've never marched up to the altar before. After all, we've been there a thousand times in the movies. From *Four Weddings and a Funeral, Love Story* to *Father of the Bride, My Big Fat Greek Wedding, Stella Dallas, June Bride, Royal Wedding*, and hundreds of others, we've seen the ministers flub the lines, the best man lose the ring, the bridesmaids weep and the bride look radiant. Is there a girl who couldn't imagine herself as Marlene Dietrich kneeling in front of the candles, the light manipulated to highlight her cheekbones, her white veil fragile (and, I imagined, flammable—always a gothic touch to my fantasies) in the flickering light?

Hollywood may have left its mark on us, as it imprinted the ideas of institutionalizing commitment into a ceremony so glorious real life could never compete. This is the tyranny of tradition; the idea that there is a standard which can only survive if we force ourselves to its mold, rather than ask it to reflect the variety of our true lives. And for decades we've done the hesitation step down the aisle of "traditional values" to a beat that is, at best, borrowed, blue and largely inauthentic.

Before movies, not all brides wore white, engagement jewelry was varied and only sometimes involved a ring (which was not called an engagement ring), teams of bridesmaids were a relatively new invention, created in pageants as ladies-in-waiting to onstage queens. But movies made our history *seem* more real than fact could ever do, and the rest of popular culture followed.

the social revolution of the sixties created options for more personal ceremonies

By the end of the Second World War, everyone wanted to return to a normalcy that had never really existed; and the pageants and events that marked our lives in America became more rigid and socially specific in the name of tradition and a desire to move to safer ground, after waves of immigration, the stock market crash, a depression, and two bloody wars.

The fifties and early sixties solidified the image of the American Wedding: a Norman Rockwell father with a pretty, strawberry-blond daughter, dressed like a freshly baked meringue. Here was a girl happy to be "given away."

If you were neither young nor strawberry-blond, if there was no father to walk you down an aisle, if you'd been to the altar before, if you wondered what to do with "his children" during a ceremony that suggested your old lives were over, or if, heaven forbid, you were dismayed by the phrase "given away," you were, indeed, the odd man out. The spectacle of a wedding was not for you and if you didn't know it, you'd be told.

No doubt you'd do something else, something suitably quiet and subdued, and you would find a way to restrain your utter delight in finding someone who loved you in spite of your obvious flaws. Some of us remember the gossip in the back of churches about whether or not the bride was entitled to wear white. This is within living memory.

Still, thirty years ago or so, the ground began to shift. In the late 1960s, young people began to question authority, institutions, presidents, parents and everything that came before. To my mind, the whole idea of opening up the discussion was a good thing; even if some of the solutions were frivolous and some of the positions as judgmental and limiting as those they attempted to replace. Couples considered living together as a viable option to marriage, basically forcing society to accept the fact. And those who married, however, began to fiddle with the vows.

"I promise to leave you space, if you leave me space" was said at one wedding I attended. And I remember another, where the bride and groom talked about "respecting their essences." What, asked my bewildered father when the wedding was over, had they promised? Silly as they might have seemed, the new rites were well intended, and the idea of standing in front of one's community to promise something personal and true was seen as an opportunity to pledge an authentic vow rather than spout a prescribed doctrine.

If the Age of Aquarius brought down some of the social, form-driven barriers, we could, at least, now allow ourselves the option to craft cere-monies that spoke to the heart of the matter. Not a few of us began, tentatively, to make what we promised actually stand for something we intended to try and live up to; no matter how many times we'd tried before, no matter what our disappointments or fears or the differences between our personal lives and an idea of bridal perfection. If the generations that immediately followed us were less influenced by our experimentation and originality, the Generation Y age bracket seems to be open to looking once again at the form and content of ritual and weaving more authentic moments through the fabric of our lives.

Add to this our culture's general, if hard-won, acknowledgment that polite society is no longer exclusively made up of Norman Rockwell families, all white and strawberry blond with not a ripple of stress on the surface of life. We now know better; and I'd suggest that the truths we've learned are far richer and indicate far greater good than Norman Rockwell might have dreamed. But the central pageant of our lives is only catching up to the good news.

Today, we find couples who choose to marry because they love one another, not because they can't get a job if they don't. They choose when and whom to marry based on love, not on what society might allow. These days we find families where divorce is met with sadness but no longer shame. And while we have a long, long way to go —gender, race, color and religion have all made their mark on what used to be a door firmly closed on social progress. As these advancements evidence social or business change, the fact that the American family is redefined by its evolution is self-evident. From two-income families at every level to extended families of exes and "formers" that make up new Theories of Relativity, there is good news to be found. And it is very different "good news" than one might have anticipated a generation ago.

We look for good news in admission policies to the top schools in the nation where they no longer observe limits on race, religion or gender, allowing women access to knowledge, friendships and careers only dreamed of by their grandmothers. We look for good news in headlines that pronounce the end of gang shootings in some urban neighborhoods, because the coupling of their residents has created a generation of mixed-culture children and communities now held together by families and love rather than racial differences. We look for good news in schools through the American heartland where the idea of an all-white, all-Protestant classroom went out with the mimeograph machine. We look for good news in the idea that we may well live to be healthy and active deep into our nineties and we should have every expectation

of finding someone else active and healthy and ready to share that life rather than the sad alternative our widowed grandparents faced in a life of solitude and decline.

We need to invent celebrations that reflect the good news of real life: the union of different cultures and different religions and different ages as pageants and rituals that strengthen our society. We need to find formats flexible enough to take entire, messy, mixed-lot families from past and present commitments into the fold and try to make warm, embracing, generous sense of them.

If you can pull it off, you have a new landscape of spiritual, intellectual and emotional possibility to set your mark, like a flag in the sand of time with your guests, your family and your community. If you can pull it off, you have one more piece of a healthier, more open, tolerant, accepting, honest, generous society to live in. Is it simple? It is not. But here are some experts who guide the way and some couples who led by example and who have forged trails and paths you may want to travel.

Debbie and David Bain each brought to their relationship children and in-laws, commitments and friends from past marriages. All the elements of lives fully lived and held close for comfort (taken and given) were noted and treasured.

Family is so clearly the concept they each hold most dear. All their children, from all of their unions, had a welcome and prominent place in their lives; and when they began living together, their home had such a mix of boys and girls under one roof that their phone numbers were listed as DAVID BAIN, REAL ESTATE, DAVID AND DEBBIE BAIN and BAIN CHILDREN.

They are each attractive, positive and bright, with great humor and energy, and a base of common sense you may not have seen since Eisenhower. That they think of themselves as lovers is certainly true; as professionals—a nurse and owner of one of Connecticut's most respected real estate brokerages—but most of all, they think of themselves as parents. The health and well-being of their children is how they measure success and their place in the world. It is yet another example we found of couples who establish the deepest connections in shared values.

It is, therefore, probably not surprising that they became engaged one morning in November as children and grandchildren were arriving for Thanksgiving. This was, after all, a holiday they understood from the heart. Their news was met with delight and input from all sides.

This brings up a point we heard about everywhere. When you plan a happy event, such as a wedding, expect interference. It's natural. People love to play a part in joyful celebrations, and they bring with them their own ideas of romance and ritual. When you state your intent or openness to breaking rules, the doors to interference open wide. In all the stories we heard, and there were

many, the intervention, for the most part, seemed to fall into two camps: the Dos and the Don'ts. Sometimes you are warned away from change by those whose beliefs are based on well-worn traditions, taken as society's "rules"; while others, energized by the possibility of romance and drama, suggest the opportunity for fantasy or an idealization of an event that carries a kind of personal resonance for them, but which may have nothing to do with the couple who will marry. It's important to remember that these ideas are usually meant in the warmest of ways—to protect you from embarrassment or to encourage you to consider a higher experience. But no one knows better than you what your own values are about. Don't be persuaded to follow rules that feel intrusive, limiting or artificial. There are many ways to circumvent these with grace and if you are comfortable in the decisions you make, the people you love are likely to be comfortable too.

The other temptation may be just as strong. We want to please the people we love and those standing on the sidelines with the banners that say DO rather than DON'T can be persuasive. But don't buy into anyone else's idea of a fantasy wedding. If you want to marry on a flying trapeze, that's great; but if you are doing it for someone else, it could be a long way down.

When Debbie and David began to look at the actual elements of a traditional wedding, there were so many things that just didn't seem to fit. To begin with, there was the reality of five children, still at home, all to house, clothe and get through college. The youngest was then seven. A wedding that incorporated only their family alone would total more than seventy people. The expense of managing an event on a grand scale was not where either of them put their priorities. The idea of eloping and returning married seemed stealthy and disconnected. But it opened the conversation as to how they felt about merging their families and in this talk they realized the center of their lives and the core of their being was their families—the fact was that this ceremony was not designed, in their minds, to commit man to wife, but family to family. There would

no longer be their families, but from now on *their* family. From this point, they had a ballast, and every element of the ceremony and the reception could be judged against it.

As they reviewed their options for traditional ceremonies, all seemed to be about moving on; moving ahead into a new life, full of joy and love, perhaps, but the children and the extended families they'd built and loved had no place in the traditional ceremonies. In the traditional picture, they would stand with their backs to those they loved and they would move, albeit metaphorically, into a new life together. It was not at all the message they wanted to deliver.

Here's what they did: David and Debbie in-

vited their family to their wedding by calling them directly. It was a warm summer and they told everyone to come to the church in comfortable clothes; no dress code, no ties, no sports jackets required. In fact, Debbie remembers telling someone that they might come barefoot.

Their family filed into the church and David and Debbie greeted them with no artificial element of ritual. When all were comfortably inside, Melissa Keck, their Congregational minister, welcomed everyone with a prayer of gratefulness and inclusion. Debbie and David stood at the front of the tiny church and explained that this ceremony was actually the introduction, one to the next, of an extended but singular family. From

this day forth, they explained, they were all related; and they would watch out for one another, care for one another and relate to one another, knowing that their safety net in the world and their connection to society had grown stronger by this day. And when they stood at the altar and introduced each "member of the wedding" to the rest of the group, Debbie says that there wasn't a dry eye in the house.

David's company real estate sign was decked out for the occasion

That's what ceremonies are intended to do—to create an emotional connection between the intellectual issue of change and the deep internal life of each member of the community who will be affected by the change. It marks that day.

There were songs and poems read and sung, there were vows made and kisses all round, but there was no moment as important as the one where every person in that room knew that their lives had grown richer and fuller because of this ritual on this warm day in July.

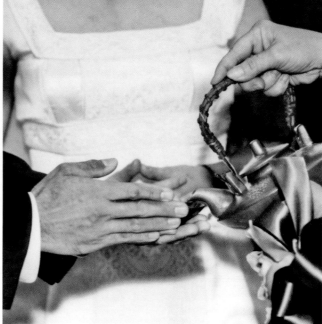

The mixing of families is, indeed, an affair to be addressed with caution and tact in doses at least as great as joy. When it involves the blending of cultures, the element of concern can be overwhelming; the best one can often hope for is that no side is offended. Dr. Fiona Gallahue and her husband, Retsu Takahashi, however, crafted a ceremony so based on love and respect that it not only managed to not offend, it was also able to transcend the cultural land mines and present a union of strength and clarity, kindness and devo-

tion in doses great enough and true enough to quiet a curmudgeon of any stripe.

Their intent to create a ceremony that honored both the Celtic heritage of Fiona and the Japanese culture of Retsu was elemental to their idea of any marriage ceremony at all. Their mix of symbols and blessings elevated the event to an authentic marriage of ways and means. There were elements of both traditions in the ceremony—from the drinking of the cups, as in Shinto ritual, to the traditional walk down the aisle and white dress.

Their officiate, the Reverand Liz Alexander, a Presbyterian minister and a close friend of the family, explained each gesture and its meaning to the guests. Martha Gallahue, Fiona's mother, and Takako Takahashi, Retsu's mother, lit a unity candle and Fiona's grandfather stood in a gesture of closure and generosity, enumerating the many similarities between the two religions, Buddhist and Christian, and their ceremonies with symbols and references that were powerful to both religions at once. In the

end, the guests all seemed to feel that the ceremony had been transcendent in a way that not only avoided the obvious possibilities for offense, but actually created an illustration of a couple who brings out the best in one another, from their talents and their feelings to their values and their individual cultures. They proved once more that there is more similar than not in things that are based in love.

Fiona and Retsu have allowed us to share their service with you. They carefully worked out their marriage ceremony, which took place at the Brooklyn Botanic Gardens in September 2004. Here they offer their ceremony in the hope that it will inspire others to see a greater connection between all people of goodwill. It is important to note that this program was written in both English and Japanese and given to their guests, so that everyone might follow.

THE BLENDED CULTURE CEREMONY
FIONA GALLAHUE AND RETSU TAKAHASHI

Fiona and Retsu carefully worked on their marriage ceremony, to be inclusive of both families' cultures and positions. They had a sensitive advocate in Reverend Alexander, who helped them to refine, clarify and amplify the meaning and intent of the rites while eliminating references that might have seemed distancing.

Prelude
Two candles will be lit representing all the members of Fiona's and Retsu's families, past and present.

Convocation
Reverend Liz Alexander
Welcome to this celebration of the marriage of Fiona Gallahue and Retsu Takahashi. We are gathered here this evening in this beautiful place to publicly witness and to bless the covenant Fiona and Retsu will make with their vows. All of us join them in celebrating this day with joy and thanksgiving.

Invocation
Let us pray. O Sacred Source of Life and Love, Creator and Sustainer, bless Retsu and Fiona with peace of heart and strength of spirit as they honor the vows they make here today. May their love for each other and their commitment to their relationship grow with each new day and fill them with understanding, kindness and strength. Amen.

Declaration of Intent
Affirmation of the couple: Retsu and Fiona, do you affirm your desire and intention to enter into this covenant of marriage and to accept the challenges, demands and joys you will face together? If so, say, We do.

Vows
It is time now, Retsu and Fiona, to share the promises you make to each other, to bind you as husband and wife.

Ceremonial Sake Blessing
An adaptation of the Shinto ceremony *san-san-su-do sakazuki-oto*, the ritual drinking of the sake in a symbolic exchange of solemn promises. It is a celebration of the heavens, earth and humankind, wishing good to all.

Presentation of Rings

What do you bring as a sign of your promise? Each ring is a symbol of the promises you have made to one another and represents the circle of your abiding love for one another.

Exchange of Rings

Fiona, I give you this ring as a symbol of my vow and a reminder of my love for you.

Retsu, I give you this ring as a symbol of my vow and a reminder of my love for you.

Lighting of the Unity Candle

At the beginning of this ceremony, two candles were lit to represent the two separate families past and present for Retsu and Fiona. Now they will light the unity candle with these two candles, not only to represent the coming together of their two separate lives, but also of all the life experiences, traditions and lessons taught to them by their families.

Wedding Prayer
Louis Ryan, grandfather of the bride

Pronouncement of Marriage

Those whom the Divine Spirit has joined together let no one separate. Fiona and Retsu, you have expressed your love and commitment for one another and have made your solemn promises to each other before your community of friends and family tonight. Therefore, by the powers vested in me, I proclaim that you are now husband and wife.

Benediction: An Irish Blessing

May the road rise before you,

May the wind be always at your back

May the sun shine warm upon your face,

The rain fall soft upon your fields

And, until we meet again,

May God hold you in the palm of his hand

this page:

Fiona and Retsu

opposite page:

Rev. Liz Alexander

officiated at

Fiona and Retsu's

wedding

Reverend Rosemary Bray McNatt, minister of Fourth Universalist Society in New York City, reminds us that we are walking a thin line when we integrate parts of other cultures into our new rituals.

"Integrate," she says, never "imitate." There is an appetite for spiritual expression these days that often goes beyond the limits of an individual's background. While there are many beautiful things to learn from other cultures and other religions, Reverend McNatt emphasizes that we should be very careful to not simply appropriate the rites of others, but, rather, to use them in proper context and with respect, as they were so intended.

Reverend Rosemary McNatt and Reverend Alison Miller are both Unitarian ministers. We met to discuss the trends, concerns, challenges

and potential joys in creating New American Wedding ceremonies; those that stretched tradition, mixed cultures or races and defied the limits of the past.

In the spirit of complete disclosure I will tell you that I also grew up as a Unitarian/Congregationalist and I admit to a bias—that these deist churches (Unitarian, Universalist and Congregational), the churches of the founding fathers, were established in a spirit of tolerance. The ability to respect others' ideas about life and death, God or gods, and hereafters of all kinds is what took our forefathers out of England to a land that was supposed to stand for something better. Something inclusive. And so it's no surprise that Unitarian ministers are often the first in line to be called when two people who love one another come to marriage from different religions and different cultures.

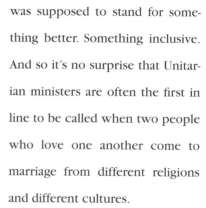

Rosemary and Alison officiate at many mixed cultural marriages and see great challenges and equally fulfilling opportunities for couples who have the courage to illustrate their love with the blending of religions and cultures. But don't assume that all members of the clergy will be eager to serve your needs, be compliant to your vision and sensitive to the wishes of each side of your family. Some will refuse to officiate if you marry outside of your faith. Many more will refuse to officiate if you wish to marry outside of their own churches, or if you wish to create your own vows, include secular music or any element that is not within their traditional and sacred ceremony.

It is important, if you want to create your own ritual, that you are prepared to do your homework and interview potential officiates at

length, long before the invitations are in the mail. Otherwise you risk being railroaded into a ceremony that holds no comfort or resonance for you or your partner.

If having the officiate as a member of the clergy is central to your idea of marriage, have faith; there are open-minded, creative members of almost every sect and religion, and with fortitude and luck, you will find one who supports your vision for a more personal and authentic service. I've known clergy to climb sand dunes and stand ankle deep in the ocean, balance on a tar rooftop in Manhattan, and throw open a church, long closed and abandoned.

Convincing a member of the clergy to wade into the sea and marry you, however, may not be the whole task. In her book, *I Do—A Guide to Creating Your Own Unique Wedding Ceremony*, Sydney Barbara Metrick suggests that you take a

this page:

The Stone Church,

New Preston, Connecticut

opposite page:

top: Reverend Allison Miller

bottom: Reverend Rosemary

Bray McNatt

close look at the actual texts of traditional ceremonies to discover whether or not the language used and the practices suggested are such that you can be comfortable with them.

For instance, many traditional ceremonies pronounce the couple man and wife, rather than husband and wife, suggesting the original idea of ownership. And if you care to be thin-skinned about such things consider the fact that until Ireland entered the legal systems of the European Union, just within the last decade, wives in that country were legally considered chattel, the definition of which is a movable possession.

Today here at home, there are traditional ceremonies where the groom promises to cherish and the bride promises to obey. "Who gives this woman?" is asked by the traditional minister, reading his text. "I do," says the father. With the advancement of the women's movement came the option of a new answer, "Her mother and I do," a statement that includes the female parent but does not correct the idea that the bride, presum-

ably a grown woman, is being "given away."

The standard Anglican ceremony is based on the 1945 edition of The Book of Common Prayer. It states unequivocally that the union is an "honorable estate instituted by God, signifying the mystical union that is betwixt Christ and his church." Along with the advice that marriage be entered into "reverently, discreetly, advisedly and soberly," it adds, "and in the fear of God."

There are many reasons why you might be comfortable with this. You might believe it. Or you may find reassurance in the traditional language of a ceremony you grew up hearing; a ceremony that was word for word the one that bound your parents, grandparents or brothers and sisters. Or possibly you believe that words do not really matter; that thinking, rational people are capable of differentiating between real life and ritual. On this point, I actually agree. I think our cultural need to frantically change traditional language to meet a PC code has taken a real toll on the beauty and weight of history in a lot of congregating ritual. But this

particular ceremony is actually supposed to be about the two of you. This isn't an Easter service at which you may sing a hymn or join in a group prayer.

If you have a degree of discomfort with any part of any traditional ceremony and don't see within the idea of ritual the chance for a truly reflective and meaningful statement of your own beliefs as a couple, you have missed one of life's great opportunities.

I am not suggesting that you need to stray far from the straight and narrow as you explore religious or secular ways to create rituals that feel authentic to your beliefs. As an example of a traditional religious ceremony that carries the gravity and dignity of history and convention, a

Quaker wedding might be looked at for its simplicity and quiet grace. In the company of their congregation, the couple holds hands and the groom declares, "In the presence of the Lord and of this assembly, I take thee to be my wife, promising with divine assistance to be unto thee a loving and faithful husband until death shall separate us." The bride repeats the same pledge. A marriage certificate is read aloud to the congregation and signed by all who have witnessed.

As for a secular ceremony, Bill Gawel, a justice of the peace from our town in Connecticut, married us on our porch a few weeks after his men spread the annual gravel on our drive. That's a small town for you, and it was just the feeling we wanted to have.

Bill Gawell,

justice of the peace, officiates

Sarah Morris wed Jeffrey Michael on Saturday, November 6, 2004, at the Brattle Theater in Cambridge, Massachusetts. If you've never heard of a wedding in a movie theater, this might open up a whole new range of possibilities.

The idea of staying in Cambridge was an essential part of their planning. And it points out the two main themes we heard in our conversations with New American couples: home and away. There was, for the most part, no in between. Most couples we spoke to wanted to celebrate at home on their own land, in their own living rooms, on their own porches, in their own towns, whether a tiny village on the side of a mountain or the middle of Brooklyn. It is a choice about staking the claim and presenting "where we live" in the truest sense of the word.

The balance chose to position their venue as a destination that was, most of all, away. In other words, "where we live in our imaginations"—as examples, the spot some think of as the most magnificent site on the Hudson River, or the magical inspiration and personal resonance of Venice. But home or away, if the choice is made consciously and carefully, they each hold wonderful possibilities for connection.

Sarah and Jeffrey called Cambridge home and wanted Harvard Square to be as central to the wedding activities as it was to their lives. The Brattle Theater has a wonderful, independent spirit. It's quirky, youthful, invested in discovering The New, but with a sense of history, and it's central (geographically and emotionally) and in many ways, at least for Sarah and Jeffrey, the essence of Harvard Square.

Sarah wrote about movies for the *Boston Globe* and the *Boston Phoenix*. She and Jeff spent their first dates at the Brattle and still occasionally manage to squeeze a double feature into their busy lives.

You can see how they worked out their choice of venues; they identified the points that were important to both of them: location and character. They then set about identifying the options within those parameters. The Brattle Theater was at the top of their list.

The bonuses of this venue were many. Most of all, it allowed Sarah and Jeffrey to "put on a show," which is exactly what pageants are—shows. The theater had a rear projection system, so no shadow is cast on the screen if one stands on the stage. It also held the possibility of rear-projected images to set an atmospheric and evocative setting. In this case, Michigan's Cranbrook Academy of Art held meaning to both Sarah and Jeff, as well as their families, and Jeff's picture of Cranbrook on a foggy morning set a scene of misty beauty and reunion. Sarah and Jeff also love black and white musicals

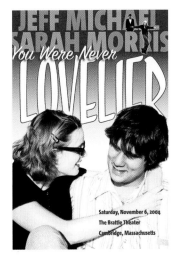

and find the dance numbers romantic beyond anything our age has produced. They secured a dance number from an Astaire–Hayworth movie and ran it at half speed for a romantic and dreamy backdrop to their event.

Sarah and Jeffrey's wedding apparel, and those of their attendants, took the black and white look of the screen into account as all was gray, white, and blue.

While much of their service is so specific to the events and nature of their lives, the welcome by their officiate, J. Tevere MacFadyen, gives you such a window into their personalities, we decided to share it here. We also include the intention and rings segment as we find it directional and generous. Additionally, Elizabeth Rehfeld, Sarah's adviser at Harvard, read from Robert Louis Stevenson and poet Kevin Young read a poem of his own composition. Sarah and Jeffrey allow us to include these parts of their service as inspiration for all.

THE SILVER SCREEN CEREMONY
SARAH MORRIS AND JEFFREY MICHAEL

Sarah and Jeffrey chose to be married on the stage of a movie theater that was personally resonant to them. It is no surprise, then, that their ceremony was also unique and personal. Their officiate was a friend and colleague who invited the guests to join in honoring Sarah and Jeff's commitment with "enthusiasm, laughter and delight." He spoke about how a decision to marry allows unimagined closeness and strength in adversity, but also the trust to encourage individual growth. Their exchange of vows and rings was especially simple, direct and touching.

Vows and Exchange of Rings

Jeff and Sarah: I ask you now to affirm your willingness
to enter into marriage by speaking the words that symbolize
the intermingling of your lives.

Jeff, do you take Sarah to be your wife? Will you love her faithfully,
with patience and understanding through life's highs and lows?
Will you strive to navigate your mutual adventure with humor and optimism?
Will you cherish and honor her now and forever? ("I will.")

Sarah, do you take Jeff to be your husband? Will you love him faithfully,
with patience and understanding through life's highs and lows?
Will you strive to navigate your mutual adventure with humor and optimism?
Will you cherish and honor him now and forever?("I will.")

"I give you this ring as a token of my love and a symbol of my commitment
to be your partner and husband/(wife) today, tomorrow and always."

Poetry and readings can also bring a sense of ceremony and depth to a wedding. Sarah and Jeffrey had friends who shared both with them and their guests and we include them here to inspire you to create new work or mine the bounty of literature and poetry to find ways to express your own true feelings.

An Excerpt from "Virginibus Puerisque"
by Robert Louis Stevenson

The essence of love is kindness; and indeed it may be best defined as passionate kindness.

That people should laugh over the same sort of jests, and have many an old story between them which time cannot wither nor custom stale, is a better preparation for life, by your leave, than many other things higher and better sounding in the world's ears. You could read Kant by your self, if you wanted, but you must share a joke with someone else.

Ere you marry, [you] should have learned the mingled lesson of the world: that hope and love address themselves to a perfection never realised, and yet, firmly held, become the salt and staff of life; that you yourself are compacted of infirmities,..., and yet you have something in you lovable and worth preserving; and that, while the mass of mankind lies under this scurvy condemnation, you will scarce find one but, by some generous reading, will become to you a lesson, a model, and a nobel spouse through life.

"Duet"
by Kevin L. Young

Let us begin

by being free.

Then, to know just

what we need—

Night without

a light

The dark

full of dream.

And you & I, I

& you, & all

the letters in between.

Andrea Giardino, one of New York's most creative party planners, once managed a wedding that had many of us a bit concerned. The couple in question wanted to stage a voodoo ceremony, and the idea of black magic seemed less than celebratory. Nothing, it seems, could have been further from the truth.

The bride, a maker of documentary films, was marrying an artist. The wedding was taking place in their loft and Andrea had devised a Caribbean feast and a jungle of palm trees, orchids and hibiscus.

A voodoo priestess, dressed in flowing white robes, conducted the ceremony, and led the guests in chants and the couple in their vows. There were drums and music, chanting and raised voices. After the exchange of rings, all of those in attendance were led to say:

"By the power vested in us as your family of friends, we now pronounce you partners for life and love."

"Honor," "respect" and "love" chants rose with the recessional drums of passion. Andrea says that while it had promised to be an unusual event, in reality it was one of the most moving and celebratory weddings she'd ever attended.

Regardless of whether it's a voodoo wedding or a promise on a beach, each state has its own laws and rules for the legalities that institute a marriage. In fact, there are states where the rules can change from county to county. Make sure that you check with your local town office before you assume anything about your wedding, as the licensing of an officiate, the age of the bride and groom, the waiting time between license and marriage, the need for blood tests, the clearing of past partnerships, the residency records of the bride and groom—all of these can be called into question. And if you are heading for a destination wedding, remember, we are not just talking about rules in different countries; do not assume that every state or every town in America has the same rules.

As ministers who endorse the idea of marriage and of authentic ceremony, Rosemary and Alison also make the point that when a couple chooses to break the rules of any traditional rite, the ceremony itself may be fraught with land mines as each side attempts to mitigate the family issues that changes in format or content can bring to the event.

In some cases they see themselves in the position of acting as advocates for the couple. But there is no doubt that the rituals deeply considered and detailed to reflect the nature and values of the couple can be more moving for partici-

pants and guess and, perhaps, more sustaining for the couple and their close community.

The more self-assured the couple, the more mature and level, the fewer the problems, they observe. Though Rosemary adds that while the challenges behind the scenes may be no less, the issues the couple allows to affect them are limited and better managed.

They also point out that the way a couple negotiates the details of their ceremony is very telling about the ways they will negotiate the issues of their life together.

Anne Watkins's wedding painting

this page:

Diana McSpadden and Rick Todd

with their dog

opposite page:

the couple

walks a petal-strewn path

following pages:

family and friends officiate

at the ceremony

Diana McSpadden and Rick Todd were a couple who had thought about their life together, their relationships with their families and their place on the planet. When they married in Vail, Colorado, they knew they wanted a ceremony that incorporated nature, the mountains and the reasons they'd chosen Vail as the place they wanted to spend their lives together. They were also set to avoid a ceremony that felt in any way false.

Here are Diana's own words, which echoed the sentiments of so many of the brides I spoke with:

"Our major concern was to have a meaningful ceremony that did not add any elements that we felt hypocritical about. I have been to many a wedding where I knew that the bride and groom found much of the service trite or insincere, or even insulting. We did not want to fall into any of those traps."

With a level of confidence of style so personal and self-assured, Diana and Rick staged a wedding that spoke to the heart of their beliefs and their love for nature, their families and each other. Rick and Diana walked up a path strewn with flower petals and were married by their "audience."

THE POWER OF THE PEOPLE CEREMONY
DIANA McSPADDEN AND RICK TODD

The guests gathered on a hillside and were greeted by Diana's stepfather, who offered this welcome:

Larry McSpadden:

We have gathered to celebrate the marriage of Rick and Diana. They are glad for your presence as they celebrate a rite as old as any in human history that we know. You are witnesses to their words and actions today. You are also the people who have taught them the meaning of love and friendship, the very things that bring them together before you. As we hear their words of commitment to each other, we will affirm the joy we feel in the beauty and the promise of the choice made by Rick and Diana to stand together all the days of their lives.

Everyone:

Rick and Diana, we ask you now to affirm your willingness to enter the marriage covenant, to speak the words that are important expressions of the intermingling of your lives.

Rick, do you take Diana to be your wife? Will you love her faithfully, with patience and understanding as you meet together life's pleasures and adversities? Will you cherish her in sickness and in health, through time of happiness and travail all the days of your life?

Rick says I do and then places the ring on Diana's finger and says:

I give you this ring as a sign that I chose you for love, to be your partner and husband today, tomorrow and always.

Everyone:

Diana, do you take Rick to be your husband? Will you love him faithfully, with patience and understanding, as you meet together life's pleasures and adversities? Will you cherish him through sickness and in health, through times of happiness and travail all the days of your life?

Diana says I do and places a ring on Rick's finger and says:

I give you this ring as a sign that I chose you for love, to be your partner and wife today, tomorrow and always.

Everyone:

By the giving and receiving of rings, you take to yourselves the relation of wife and husband. You came today as two single people and you leave as a married couple, united by the vows you have exchanged. The best of good fortune to you both.

The Wedding of Helen Diana McSpadden and Richard

axophone courtesy of John Vogel

Larry McSpadden Welcomes Guests

Readings by Larry and Jane McSpadden

Mothers Speak
Susan Vogel
Anne Todd

Readings by the Sisters
Kate Todd
Laura LeCount

Readings by the Fathers
Chuck Sams
Thomas Todd

Thomas Todd leads the guests in the wedding vows

Everyone: Rick and Diana we ask you now to affirm your
eak the words that are important expressions of the inte
take Diana to be your wife? W
life's pleasures an

this page:

Clare Henry and Phillip Bruno

at their marriage ceremony

in the Louise Nevelson-

designed chapel

at Saint Peter's Church

opposite page:

top: their kiss

bottom: posing before the cross at

Saint Peter's Church

Clare Henry and Phillip Bruno had three destination receptions: New York, Scotland and France, but only one wedding. Because their lives are almost completely defined by love and art, Clare Henry and Phillip Bruno married in the chapel of the Good Shepherd of Saint Peter's Church in New York City. For those of you who might never have visited, this church is connected at street level to the Citicorp Building and famously involved with the arts, both visual and performing. Their jazz services are world renowned and their art collection and, indeed, the building and details of the church itself have been designed by many famous artists.

As a part of their activities, the community of Saint Peter's encourage permanent works of art as a part of their worship experience. Phillip Bruno is on their review committee and helps to guide their purchases and vet their exhibitions as Saint Peter's attempts to fulfill its art ministry by expanding their own collection and offering their galleries to provoke dialog among people of New York City regarding the nature and scope of art's spiritual qualities.

The chapel of the Good Shepherd at Saint Peter's Church is a breathtaking sculptural environment created by the eminent American sculptor Louise Nevelson. Measuring only twenty-one feet by twenty-eight feet, the chapel is a five-sided space with sculptural elements of white

THE SIGNIFICANCE OF THE SETTING, SURROUNDED BY WORLD-CLASS ART, CREATED A RITE OF GREAT RESONANCE FOR THE COUPLE.

painted wood on white walls. The cross of the Good Shepherd is white paint and gold leaf. Floors, pews, and altar are bleached ash. The window is frosted white.

The ceremony was, for the most part, traditional and incorporated readings by their respective children, including a poem written for Clare by the American poet Samuel Menashe and a poem Clare had written to Phillip. The significance of the setting, surrounded by world-class art, in an environment of such personal meaning to Phillip, created a rite of great resonance for the couple and their family. They encourage you to seek the places of your heart, the spots that best express the values you uphold and the beauty you recognize.

That Ron Gold and Sara Hudson married on a Hudson River site is poetic. But it is the place Ron always imagined he would marry Sara. Like her name, it is redolent of history and romance. Ron played the flute and led the procession, of Sara's daughter, niece and nephew, and then Sara herself, who all followed his music to the gathering place. They incorporated both minister and rabbi in their ceremony and very close to the spot where he asked her to marry him, they became husband and wife, surrounded by friends and family, as the sun set on the river.

Sara made a crucial point about the importance of ritual. She and Ron thought long and hard about the expense and the work, the attention to detail and disruption to their lives a wedding would cause. They were realistic and tossed the ideas back and forth many times. But, she says,

the fact that they were not young reminded them that the people they loved and the people who loved them might not be around forever. It was a chance to bring families together and to celebrate the whole idea of being a clan: the family of birth and the family you choose. As time would have it, Sara and Ron each lost parents shortly after the wedding and came to appreciate having taken the chance of celebration all the more.

this page:

niece and nephew of the bride make their way down the stairs

both rabbi and minister officiated at the ceremony
overlooking the Hudson River

opposite page:

Ronald Gold plays the recorder and leads the
procession at his marriage to Sara Hudson

this page:

a fairy flautist led

the procession

a bridesmaid is a

Renaissance princess

opposite page:

Nic's first vows were to

Hanna, Matt's daughter,

here dressed as

"Best Butterfly"

the attendants were dressed

in all manner of

fantasy finery

Perhaps the most extraordinary ceremony we came across was that of Nic York and Matt Bogen. Their wedding in Los Angeles was over the top in many ways, but as fun and free as it seems, the underpinnings were strong and deep and heartfelt.

The idea of Dress Up came about through an early longing for masquerade, but developed into a chance to allow Nic's attendants to fulfill their own fantasies. The idea of dressing together for an event in which they would all star was a gift Nic could give to her friends. Their effort was a gift they gave back to her.

The music played as they walked down the aisle of the restored grand hotel space they'd found was the music from Cirque du Soleil's "O," haunting and mysterious and as far from Wagner as one might find.

As part of the vows, Nic began with a vow to Hanna to be a good and loving stepmother, to listen and to laugh and always be willing to go shopping. She presented Hanna with a butterfly necklace instead of a ring.

And the vows to Matt included a reading from her journal the morning after their first date, where she wrote not only about how dear and sweet he was but about how much she enjoyed the salmon entrée. Her point, of course, is that even then she knew this moment with Matt was important enough to record.

They invented a Ceremony of the Hands and told one another, as they were giving hands in marriage, what each of their hands meant to them—how strong, how comforting, how beautiful. The wedding party walked up the aisle instead of down, led by a flautist dressed as a fairy.

The flowers were as inventive as the concept and supported the masquerade choices of the bridesmaids—a flower snake for Eve, flowers in Rapunzel's hair. Matt's daughter, Hanna, was Best Butterfly and wore wings.

By anyone's definition, I suppose, Nic and Matt created a fantasy wedding, but it was based on a foundation of truth with such inspired sincerity, goodwill and good intention that it seems to me now to be anything but fantasy. Such is the stuff of real life and love, more glorious than one can make up.

If this book suggests anything, I hope it is the power of finding your own voice in ritual and trusting that its clarity can move the planet along, even in a tiny nudge, toward the unique way the two of you see a world made richer, kinder and fuller through love.

CHAPTER 9

THE RECEPTION

BECAUSE WEDDING CEREMONIES HAVE BEEN, UNTIL NOW,

JUST WHAT PEOPLE EXPECTED THEM TO BE, WHAT MOST

PEOPLE MEAN WHEN THEY THINK ABOUT OR TALK ABOUT

A WEDDING IS THE WEDDING RECEPTION.

This was the part the guests could get into, and this was the part where the time and the effort and the money all worked or didn't work, as the case might be. I'd managed a lot of events for clients and I was not shy about throwing a party. But what made a party a wedding? And what made a wedding reception "New American" rather than traditional?

When my mother planned her own wedding reception at her family's town club more than sixty years ago, it never occurred to her that someone like Robert Isabell might transform the staid and conservative room into a czar's palace, or that a 1940s' version of Preston Bailey could create a Venetian canal, complete with gondolas, in the foyer of the Union Club on the East Side of Manhattan.

Had anyone suggested it, she would have smiled politely and moved away. It just wasn't done. Wealthy parents might splurge on a dazzling wedding dress, or plan a reception at the Plaza Hotel instead of a family club, but weddings staged like a chapter from the tales of Ara-

bian Nights, with projected photos of minarets at sunset, silver platters piled high with ortolan and elephants leading the bridal procession were things that belonged to a pasha or a movie star. In contrast, picnics or potluck dinners would have struck them as something that Daisy Mae and Li'l Abner might have cooked up for their wedding, and no one in my parents' set would have seen the reason, wit or even any humor in the choice.

Times changed a little by the 1970s, and my mother and I hung from the rafters and helped to dress a friend's barn for her wedding. But with huge balls of daisies and greens hanging from the beams, and swags of flower-studded bowers draped along the stalls, the barn was neither transformed into a pasha's tent nor a Parisian nightclub. It might have been dressed, but it was still a barn. A tent ran from the far door and housed the dance band and the buffet. My mother had the idea of wrapping the poles with corn husks—a trick Zeze and I repeated thirty years later at my own Connecticut wedding.

Sometime between then and now, some level of wedding receptions for some level of society have become theater. Venues have become movie sets and all manner of opulence is considered. I've actually heard tales of a bride who appeared on a cloud of dry ice, one who swung down on a Fragonard swing, and another who entered from behind a long walkway of scrim so that she was in silhouette for the first minutes of her walk down the aisle. It all sounds more like the Ziegfeld Follies; but after countless interviews with all kinds of couples, from all walks of life, New American Weddings just don't seem like that to me. The wedding receptions we're talking about might be as elegant and heady as a Casanova ball or down home as a potluck supper, but the celebration is more likely to be about reality than fantasy.

When it comes to the reception, however, even reality is going to take its toll. I promise, when you review every detail you'll need to invent, control, present and pay for, it will be enough to make you consider running for a lad-

der to elope. And maybe that's a good idea. Sometimes knowing that you don't want what will amount to a high level of stress, expense and intensity of emotion is a fair response to the idea of publicly tying the knot. No one here will tell you that you can't send out pretty announcements and call it a day.

But if you want a celebration, don't let anything dissuade you from your moment. There is joy to be had at every budget and for every personality. So square your shoulders, keep your chin up and remember, it may be the greatest chance you're given to express yourself as a couple and be surrounded by people who love you and wish for your happiness.

As a note, if you suspect that some of the folks on the first draft of your guest list don't feel that way about you, you might want to reconsider inviting them. One of the trends in New American Weddings is that couples don't have to invite people who don't care a fig about them.

This is your wedding, not your parents', and the clients of your father or a clutch of cousins

who have been obvious in their disdain for family events through the years needn't be included. Receptions should be open and warm, amounting to the gift you give back to your family and friends. Choose your guests as carefully as you choose the way you want to express yourself, and you will be well on the way to a glorious time.

Many good books exist with advice for managing wedding receptions, from the wonders of do-it-yourself with *The Handcrafted Wedding* to a charming book filled with lovely seasonal examples called *The Perfect Wedding Reception* to a pull-out-the-stops Preston Bailey's *Fantasy Weddings*. There are brilliant ideas, solid hints, well-thought-out checklists, stunning pictures, menus—all kinds of options

to consider. We don't need to reiterate them here, but even in the most basic of these books, right up front, they give you advice like "Reception details are dictated by the location." And it's good advice; don't try to make a barn into a winter palace, it suggests. But it doesn't tell you whether or not you should want a winter palace, or a barn. These books don't tell you how to determine what it is that speaks most eloquently for you.

How different is that skill—the art of creating an event that is just for you, something much more personal, quirky, creative; something that bases its resourcefulness on individuality rather than on how much money or effort or detail or beauty one might throw at a party?

For the Bednar–Long wedding reception, I'd suggest that the overriding idea that makes this a New American Wedding is the fact that everything, from the location to the cocktail napkin, was chosen as a personal reflection of a personal style. Almost like a merchandising campaign, Susan Bednar and John Long used favorite colors and stripes to act the way a logo might act in retail. They chose a location that was important to them, shared their favorite foods, gave gifts of music that had personal meaning. It was as though they invited friends and family into a private world where they were in total control of the kingdom.

When Susan considered the details of her

wedding reception, the idea of staging it in Italy had already been decided in conversations with John, her soon-to-be husband, as a destination they loved and could share with their friends and family. What she knew she wanted out of the reception was an evening that could only have been theirs. As a designer, she wanted her stamp, her taste, her colors and patterns on everything everyone saw.

Their sense of play as a couple and Susan's attention to detail created an event that transcended the usual reception in many ways. Susan loves stripes; as an interior designer, she calls it her "signature." For this event, she called up stripes galore; from the cocktail napkins and

this page and opposite:

the Italian reception of

Susan Bednar

and John Long

dessert pastries, waiters' bow ties and the striped ribbons in the centerpieces to the tablecloths of jacquard pale gray stripes and the dinner menus designed with striped teal borders. Add to this Susan's love of aqua, turquoise and all things teal, and you have an idea of where this reception was going from a design point of view.

The food at those pretty settings made the best of the Italian wedding tradition of a five-course meal and included salmon and swordfish tartare, veal medallions and vegetable risotto. Their wedding favors were the couple's favorite love songs, packaged in a striped jacket cover with a photo of a Venetian palazzo that uses stripes in its stonework.

The band was Italian but played a mix of American rock and roll with their Italian popular music. Susan and John sang their favorite song, a duet called "Here's to Love" from the movie *Down with Love* and then danced all night. All in all, it was a party planned and controlled right down to the last sugared almond to feature the likes and loves of a couple delighted with the whole idea of being in love and sharing their happiness with friends.

The Henry–Bruno wedding reception provided yet another brilliant reflection of their life together in a world of art. As art critic and journalist, Clare, and Phillip, the curator, gallery director and mentor to some of America's most renowned artists, saw every detail and every choice as an opportunity to celebrate the fact that art is almost always within reach, if we just think to reach out and touch it.

At Clare and Phillip's New York reception, the walls of a friend's working-artist loft were completely collaged as a One-Night-Only art installation. As presents and souvenirs, artist/guests created drawings and pieces of art.

And then when it was done and packed up and paid for, they did it again and again, in what sounds like the Wedding Reception Tour. Because their family and friends scattered the

globe, Clare and Phillip staged parties in France and Scotland for all of those dear who could not travel to New York. In Glasgow, Clare found an artist who could faithfully silk-screen photographic images onto cakes. She had a cake created to showcase her own image in her bright, New York wedding dress, right on the top, for those who had missed the moment.

As a wonderful bonus, Clare's daughter, Zara, had flown into New York with her boyfriend to attend her mother's wedding and became engaged the very next day, on the observation deck of the Empire State Building. So, for the party in Glasgow, Clare had the cake artist whip up a second cake with an image of the Empire State Building, to share the celebration.

Where did the idea of the personalized wedding begin to take over the braver and the more self-possessed bride? The first place I was aware of seeing a high degree of creativity and personal expression in weddings at all was in the unlikely category of "The Cake." Could this possibly be true?

I knew of one real expert to confirm the theory—the doyenne of wedding cakes, Sylvia Weinstock. Sylvia, after all, was mentioned in Martha Stewart's first wedding book and has appeared in nearly every magazine and article on creative weddings since. Her cakes have been featured in every possible relevant publication and often form the centerpiece of celebrity wedding coverage. They are inventive, often witty, wildly expensive and, most important, beautifully executed examples of edible art.

She has, therefore, an overview of whether we're seeing a trend, this idea that the wedding cake can be an expressive element of the couple—their life, their taste, their cultures.

Not only does she confirm it, Sylvia believes that weddings in general are much more expressive of personal taste and individuality than ever before. As early as ten years ago (her business is twenty-five years old), she started to sense an appreciation for cakes that were more unique.

"Often, the cake was the only thing about the wedding where the bride and groom allowed themselves to break out of the mold a little."

Eureka! Early evidence of the New American Wedding.

Pictures of Sylvia's work of-art wedding cakes for celebrities like Bryant Gumbel, Mariah Carey, Robert DeNiro and Donald Trump line her walls, as do

this page:

a wedding cake

bedecked with butterflies;

Sylvia Weinstock in the kitchen

opposite page:

an Indian bride;

the henna-decorated

hands of a bride;

and a wedding cake by

Sylvia Weinstock

with henna pattern

the framed profiles of her business from *Town and Country, Departures, InStyle* and *People*. Some of the cakes seem more traditional than others, but none are run of the mill. All express an exuberant idea of style that goes way beyond the expected.

Sylvia neither works with nor endorses fondant, a heavy, inedible clay of sugar that coats so many wedding cakes; her cakes are more fragile, but even her rendition of the Leaning Tower of Pisa was delicious, by all accounts. She has also decorated a cake with a beautiful paisley hennaed pattern of an Indian bride's hand and copied the embroidery from a gown onto the surface of a cake. Sylvia created what looks like a crate of wine for a couple who owns vineyards, complete with bottles and bunches of grapes—all cake. And she constructed a completely edible and spectacular version of an ancient Chinese

woven basket overflowing with flowers for a couple who was active in the Asia Society. A wedding in a conservatory suggested a fanciful greenhouse cake and a ceremony at the Botanical Gardens' Butterfly House inspired a cake with fluttering butterflies lighting on the smooth surface delicate as a summer garden in a fairy tale.

These confections' price tags can run to the thousands of dollars and could equal the cost of indigestible art hanging on a gallery wall, but my guess is that no guest will ever forget a cake surrounded by what appears to be live butterflies and flowers. If you can manage the sticker price and give Sylvia a theme, a piece of fabric, a wish or a dream, you've got yourself a delicious piece of one-of-a-kind magic.

Whether she bakes the cake or not, Sylvia offers a tip: "Embrace the challenge of design and coordinate your cake to the rest of the event."

THE WALDORF-ASTORIA
RED VELVET CAKE

And who says a wedding cake has to be white? Outside or inside? Nic and Matt Bogen had a cake of gleaming white and pearls on the outside, but inside it was red! The bakers followed Nic's mother's Waldorf-Astoria recipe for their red velvet cake. From the outside it was a beautiful white cake studded with candied pearls; on the inside it was blood red. Just the thing for a masquerade.

The Cake:

2 ounces red food coloring	1. Make paste of coloring and cocoa.
3 tablespoons cocoa	2. Cream shortening, sugar and eggs. Add
½ cup shortening	coloring and cocoa paste. Mix well.
1 ½ cups sugar	3. Add buttermilk with vinegar, and flour
2 eggs	with salt, alternately.
1 cup buttermilk	4. By hand, fold in vanilla and baking soda.
1 tablespoon vinegar	5. Grease and flour cake pans.
2 ¼ cups flour	Makes 3 layers.
¾ teaspoon salt	6. Bake at 350° for 30 minutes.
1 teaspoon vanilla	
1 teaspoon baking soda	

The Frosting:

	1. Cook flour and milk until thick.
3 tablespoons flour	
1 cup milk (cool)	2. Beat shortening, margarine, sugar and
½ cup shortening	vanilla until creamy.
½ cup margarine	
1 cup sugar	3. Mix together and add the milk and flour
1 teaspoon vanilla	mixture a little at a time and beat well.

I could fall into the trap of suggesting a more authentic wedding implies an inherently simpler reception, based at home ground, with little need to impress. Not true. It wasn't even true of mine, and that was on home turf and had guests dressed in jeans. But the best example I've found is that of Nic and Matt Bogen's reception.

As over the top as it might have been, the masquerade ball reception of Nic and Matt Bogen so completely captured the madcap creativity, fun and flair for drama this Los Angeles couple obviously cultivates in their lives that it offers a great example of New American Wedding thinking. From the masks worn through dinner to the fact that the candelabras on the tables became party favors to the guests who entertained and

the band that kept everyone dancing and dancing through the night to the-end-of-the-reception brunch, served in silver chafing dishes but containing all things fun, familiar and too often forbidden from McDonald's, this was an event that was so inherently Nic and Matt's.

Nic says that from the time she was a little girl, she asked for a masquerade ball and the chance never came up. Her mother speculates that if she'd given in when Nic was eleven, a wedding like this might never have happened. They and their guests would have been the poorer for it. I am sure, however, that Nic must have another longed-for experience in her bag of tricks—and could stage equally inventive, equally touching events for its base of kindness and shared, giddy joy.

this page, top:

dramatic mask

at the Bogen reception

bottom:

the bride and groom

opposite page:

the wedding cake

of Nic and Matt Bogen

*The lovely thing about most of our New American Wedding receptions is that once you know the couple, you can't imagine them having staged their receptions very differently. Of the many women we talked to about their weddings, most had slightly blanched, if not out and out balked, at the options they first thought were available to them. They'd either already lived through traditional weddings and parent-driven receptions or they'd grown out of wanting them; and the choices for their upcoming wedding receptions seemed both too great and too narrow. They came to their ideas with the natural bit of struggle that always accompanies the birth of The New. But Anne Watkins seems always to have known her direction and she always wanted to get married in the winter.

Anne not only knew how she wanted her wedding to feel, but she also knew how she wanted it to smell. She specifically wanted that very particular scent of December and early January that brings mimosa, clove and orange pomanders, fir and cedar, the soft comfort of cashmere, the idea of candles and fires and people coming together to share the warmth of a room and the warmth that's in their hearts. So, dinner at home was right in line. Snow falling was a bonus.

Anne Watkins did the unthinkable for many of us: she cooked her own wedding dinner. She's a very unusual woman. An artist who paints weddings for a living has to be someone a bit off the center track, I suppose, choosing the joy of creat-

ing over the stability of a paycheck each week. The wedding photographer, John Dolan, whose work is also featured in this book, knows her well and describes her as "light in a bottle." She could, in fact, warm a room, and often does.

If the idea of cooking a meal by yourself is - enough to make you run out in the snow barefoot, consider a caterer and let them know that you want the meal to look welcoming and homemade, rather than tortured, towered or prepped. A lot of caterers' tricks are wonderful for buffets, and I'm the last to suggest that efforts shouldn't be made to delight guests, but when the theme is all about being home, the look of the food should support it.

David and Anne's wedding menu for forty guests is all manageable, Anne assures me, with just a little planning and talent, in your own kitchen. If you are devising your own menu, she sends a few tips: Choose food that doesn't require perfect temperatures or much last-minute fussing, allow enough nonmeat food for vegetarians and, most of all, find a wonderful warm person to hire who will take charge of the kitchen. Anne says that her "find" was "the wonderful Marilyn," who pulled the roast from the oven to rest, steamed the asparagus, filled ice buckets, refreshed glasses, retrieved an escaped cat and did everything "perfectly and with a lot of laughter." The aroma from this meal must have added to the atmosphere of home and holiday, as reading it I can almost imagine the scent as the front door to Anne and David's apartment opened.

WEDDING MENU
ANNE WATKINS DAVID MILLMAN AND

Two Wines
A fizzy white from the Veneto and a luscious red from Piedmont

Dark beer, light Scotch and plenty of Perrier

Classic relish trays with radish roses

Caviar with crème fraîche and little toasts

Chilled shrimp with cocktail sauce

Lusty olives

Nuts

Ratatouille
Made a day ahead. Great vibrant colors and vivid taste.

Scalloped Potatoes
A bit of onion, and both cheddar and Gruyère make these potatoes Anne's.

Contra Filet of Beef
A shell steak roast—no bone, and a cut that was new to Anne. Recommended by her butcher, who promised it would be the best beef anyone had ever tasted and was right. Served with freshly grated horseradish.

Asparagus
With Shallot Vinaigrette

Wedding Cake
The wedding cakes were a gift from Anne's friend Barbara Smithers, who grew up on the Isle of Wight. Three cakes, actually; two walnut tarts and an English Christmas-Wedding Cake of her own design, that combined dried fruit, nuts, marzipan and cognac. They placed it on Anne's great-grandmother's round rosebud cake plate and tucked mimosa and rosemary sprigs around it.

Cookies
Another gift, homemade chocolate and butter cookies,

and bowls of Clementines sat on the table, for color and flavor

and yet one more perfect Christmas scent, for so many of us.

There were many gifts from friends, Anne reminds us. Her bouquet, flowers for the apartment of white French lilacs and another of fragrant white flowers and orange parrot tulips. An old boyfriend stepped into the job of doorman-greeter and another pal brought the coat rack. John Dolan took pictures and a friend, named Virginia, played "My Romance" on the piano. Most of all, Anne and David were at home, surrounded by their dogs and cats and friends and family. David didn't have to stand out in public and make a speech, Anne could wear her red pajamas. Their reception was just like their life—comfortable, accessible, warm, quirky, full of love and quiet beauty and the reflection and a sense of registering detail that two artists bring to their lives and, therefore, to ours.

Sarah Morris and Jeffrey Michael wanted to keep their whole wedding in Cambridge. They loved a restaurant called Upstairs on the Square, which was just a short walk from the Brattle Theater, where they staged their ceremony. It's a place of great warmth from fireplaces, vibrant colors, cheerful and accommodating owners, and it has a history of affiliation with Harvard, that made it perfect for Sarah and Jeff. Here is their tip: Lunch is often far more affordable than dinner at restau-

rant receptions. The timing also fit their Brattle Theater time slot. They allowed a meat and a fish entrée to be chosen by guests and created a Wedding Dessert Buffet with—cupcakes—just one of the many times we spotted cupcakes in our interviews. All in all, the reception was a perfect choice for all the "practical and personal" reasons, as Sarah puts it. It fit them to a tee.

THE NUTS AND BOLTS OF WEDDING PLANNING
DIXIE TODD

NAW:

Are there any guidelines on what things should cost or even how to think about prioritizing costs? There must be some—like X# of guests to Y# of servicepeople.

Dixie:

At least one serviceperson for every ten guests. After a while you know how to gauge things, you size them up very quickly. But here's a formula you can use: for dining, dancing and band, figure twenty square feet per guest.

NAW:

For table and chair rentals, what's the average cost per person?

Dixie:

Thirty-five dollars to fifty-five dollars per person, making it clear that there are less and more expensive alternatives, depending upon how creative you want to be.

NAW:

My research is suggesting that more people seem to want outdoor weddings than ever before. Are you finding this and, if so, why do you think it's happening?

Dixie:

It seems so to me, too. Perhaps I have a higher number of type A clients, and they are people who like to control their own show. At a wedding hall or hotel, the venue inevitably puts its own stamp on the event. "We always lay out the tables this way." But at one's own home or somewhere similar, the personal tastes and desires of a client can be executed without interference.

NAW:

How do you determine the suitability of outdoor weddings?

Dixie:

If anyone involved absolutely turns ashen at the mere mention of rain, outdoor weddings are not for them.

If the site is level and the parking is manageable, or guests can be ferried in minibuses (and we can dress these quite beautifully, as you know we did for your wedding) from a parking area to the tent, then we can stage a whole wedding and reception within a tent quite beautifully.

NAW:

What do you think are the most important things to get right when managing an event?

Dixie:

Planning, planning, planning, and having the very, very best staff and vendors. I hope my clients can relax and be guests/hosts at their own wedding, whether it's dinner for fifty, a party for two or a lavish event for six hundred.

Many an advertising campaign has sent me on a chase to find a location that might look like a turn-of-the-last-century greenhouse or an old-fashioned country grange, an ivy-covered cottage, an elegant library or a modern glass house. Every major city has location scouts for this kind of hunt, and owners who will lease their sites to a movie company or a commercial shoot will usually be open to renting to someone for an event. In small towns, you might consider asking the local real estate brokers for help, or paying them as consultants to find and negotiate the right place for you and your idea. Once you realize that you are not limited to the spaces and sites everyone else has used before, you can begin to think about the reception as an event to delight your guests and express the singular idea of the two of you as a couple. There are so many interesting places one might choose for a personal wedding reception that seem never to be considered as a venue. Here are a few:

If your grammar school or high school holds a kind of resonance for you, how about throwing the kind of prom you wish you'd been able to enjoy years ago, when you were too worried about your skin, your dress or the fact that Billy Decker was dancing with Peggy Moore? Ask around—I'll bet there isn't a friend who wouldn't relish spending an evening moving back in time to Motown music. The food could be retro, from bite-size burgers and paper cones of crispy hot fries to bowls of cheese doodles, spiked punch and a cake made like a *croque en busche* tower of Hostess Snowballs. In this case, it's far more about enchanting your guests with the wit of the idea than impressing them with food. Although I have to add that Andrea Giardino once created a dinner party for my company where she took iconic American packaged foods (like Twinkies) and created them with superb ingredients. It was clever, witty and deliciously wonderful. If you are in the mood to splurge, you might have an a capella doo-wop group singing in the hall as your guests arrive. But don't even think about spending much money on the decorations. The more like crepe paper and a handmade paper moon the ornaments, the sweeter the nostalgic air.

With so much interest in outdoor and casual weddings in this New American Wedding sector, we find very few couples have designed in-door options that allow the rain to fall without damage or regret. We have a few good suggestions. Many small towns have a grange hall with a big meeting room—some with working kitchens; almost every town has a church with a meeting hall and many of the early wooden churches have separate outbuildings with kitchens and wonderful small-town character.

Empty barns can be made enchanting with just a little work (and an insurance rider for the evening). The barn doesn't have to be yours, but remember, don't rent it for the weekend; rent it for the week—that's at least how long it will take to clean and decorate for the party. I love the idea of barn dances and square dances, with dinner served from cast-iron pots on enameled plates. I love the look and comfort of long tables, bandanna napkins, fried chicken, collard greens and grits. If

you can't cook at your barn dance or want to take the path of least resistance, consider having a local barbecue joint cater. Huge platters of ribs and baskets of cornbread might be just the thing for hungry two-steppers. But our tip: Think it through and get the right props and serving pieces. You won't easily find these at a party rental facility. Borrow or buy heavy, worn old platters and baskets. Pails (obviously they need to be scrupulously clean), huge wooden bowls or even the tops of barrels work brilliantly lined with gingham or bandannas to hold bread or muffins or chicken. If you can't find tin plates, try to find wholesale pie tins, or, failing that, plain, heavy white homy dinnerware. It's important to remember that the look of the serving pieces and the table settings add real punch to your theme.

Don't turn down a venue because it has no services. Most caterers have (or have access to) trailer kitchens and portable generators. Like the ultraluxurious version of the Portosan we rented for our own reception in our field, we use these movable kitchens on location shoot-

ings, too. For some reason, civilians don't seem to know these options exist—but they do—and they open up all kinds of environments: a party in the woods with campfires blazing; a tent beside a frozen pond, with a selection of ice skates in every size; or a beautiful old building in town or out that may no longer have its services in working order. Every state has a film commission that might agree to help you or your planner or caterer to find services you can bring to a site. You may not be a film company but there is no harm in asking.

Or consider planning the reception around something you and your partner want to support. Many town libraries are lovely and now, more than ever, they require fund-raising efforts to manage and expand their programs. Talk to the director of your library or the head of the library's friends committee. Your guests might make a gift to the library endowment in your name. Your entertainment might be chamber music and "readings on the theme of love" by a few local actors. There has not been a speech at any

wedding reception I've attended to top the musings on love by Keats, or Yeats, or of the Brownings—Elizabeth and Robert. A wedding in a library supports the idea of love and the written, spoken and read words that honor it.

A gallery or the studio of an artist you admire and want to support could be the scene of a great reception. You'll be surrounded by art that you love and your guests will learn more about you and be exposed to something that might lead to their own delight. You might provide Conté crayons or pastels and ask each of them to draw something on large sheets rather than to write in a book. When the reception is over, have them all framed and create a gallery wall that will remind you all of the night of your wedding and the friends who shared it with you.

There are camps or old rural hotels scattered all across the country that allow large groups to rent their facilities for weeks or weekends. While they never seem to be noted in the wedding guides, we see their names in reference to off-site corporate meetings or company recreational weekends. These kinds of environments allow big groups of families to come together without the hassles or expense of international travel. Many have a kind of rural, honest quaintness that seems to fit the look and concept so many New American couples seem to be embracing. Don't expect any level of elegance or service. As you should count on bringing in all that you require, make sure your own caterer and planner will be welcomed, or be prepared to accept the standards of the hotel or camp. This may, at first glance, seem to be part of the atmosphere you're gong for, but to my way of thinking, the level will be neither witty enough nor good enough to suggest taste or irony. You'll need to bring in your own talent. And speaking of talent, I've always liked the idea of talent shows. What about a wedding where the gifts are all performed? Someone sings, another tap dances, someone juggles, a poem is read or performed. You'll need a producer in line months before and no expectation of finding the next gold record star, but if everyone was a good sport and up for the game, wouldn't it be fun?

The thing to remember is that New American celebrations and receptions should never be done by the book. They don't need to be expensive or elaborate, but the route should always be original and always about the two of you. A New American Wedding reception should have a sense of adventure, of a road less taken, of insight and warmth and personal care. As one of our brides, Sarah Morris, noted, by not going to a tried and true venue, your work may be harder. You may need to lean on your planner, your caterer or your more creative friends to help you discover or produce the details of your celebration, but take heart—your reception will be yours and so much richer for the effort.

Debbie and David Bain took this one step further. They asked their friends and family to bring the reception with them! The "potluck" reception was a concept we heard more than once and caterer-party designer Andrea Giardino has more than a little to say about it.

MUSINGS ON "POTLUCK" RECEPTIONS
ANDREA GIARDINO

Andrea:

I think potluck is a terrible idea.

NAW:

Hmmm. All right. Interview over. (Laughter)

Andrea:

No, seriously, I don't *really* think it's completely terrible. I understand where it comes from and how much it supports a feeling of sharing and the creation of a casual and familial experience. But if it's not managed with a great degree of control, it's likely to become truly awful.

Remember, a wedding reception is really centrally about entertaining—and entertaining is more than just putting nutritious food on the table. It's a gift you give your guests.

NAW:

You are an unusual resource—a party planner who also cooks. Food, therefore, must be a crucial part of your planning?

Andrea:

I think that exceptional food is central to showing people that you really do care about them. If the environment is over the top but the food is mediocre, somehow all the decorations seem hollow, and everyone winds up talking about the rubber chicken or the tasteless cake. We've all been to those kinds of parties. And we've been to others where the food and drink were so glorious and delicious you never knew the paint was peeling!

NAW:

Do you think one can ever make potluck work?

Andrea:

Yes, but first you must know what you're starting with. Are there friends who have special recipes or dishes that they are known for? If you try to organize an event around the things that people do exceptionally well, you'll be better served than arbitrarily assigning something safe, like three-bean salad.

For instance, I once actually organized a potluck reception for the wedding of friends. And that's how I know there's a huge amount of organization required.

The groom was an old friend from Uruguay who was marrying a beautiful doctor with family from Jamaica. They are part of a larger group of friends who are all here in New York from other countries. So I figured that if each of us knew one specialty dish from their country, they could bring this to create a feast, and that would be a celebration of how we bring our cultures with us when we come to America.

Hugo, the groom, intended to wear authentic gaucho clothes—which is how I knew the idea of representing our mother countries was in his heart at this time.

I listed all the nationalities that would be represented at the wedding and made a list of all the foods those countries were known for. From there I designed the meal, with some options, and began to call the guests and assign the dishes. It was a small enough group, and that's another very important point:

potluck works best with small groups because they are easier to control.

Next I helped most of them with measurements to change their kitchen recipes to quantities that might feed thirty or forty. It's important to remember that very few home chefs are prepared to cook for more than twenty people and you don't want to offer a dish that is not sufficient in quantity to serve all.

Another important part to control is the presentation. The best place to start is to get serving dishes that are all coordinated. They don't need to be expensive but they must look as though they all belong in the same place. You can rent them or buy them. For Hugo, I got wonderful huge terra-cotta bakers and shallow bowls and dishes from a garden supply market and I distributed them to our "cooks." At Hugo's house we had all the garnishes waiting for their arrival, and the ovens were hot and ready for anything that needed to be heated before serving.

I worked out a buffet tablescape in advance and I knew where every platter and bowl would be. I made little cards for each dish so that everyone could read what the dish was, who made it and what country it came from.

Everyone loved it! They all shared recipes the night of the wedding. You know, South Americans went home with a pesto recipe from an Italian, and the woman who made the Jamaican chicken went home with my empanada recipe. One friend couldn't cook but she was a brilliant florist. As everyone else was making food, she made a cake of flowers that looked just like a real cake with a slice missing, and brought it on a cake stand.

In some ways it might have been easier to just do the food myself but it wouldn't have supported as well the essence of this group of friends. We were able to honor our home countries in this celebration that was a marriage of cultures and also suggest that the bits of our own past that came with us were still able to enhance and enrich our new lives.

NAW:

So, if I'm getting it, potluck can work but it should be a natural element of the wedding theme. It needs tight, detailed organization and planning, spectacular design and a high degree of cooperation from the participants.

Andrea:

Yes. If it's not going to look slipshod it needs all of those things. And I think there are very few places where it is appropriate, but when it is and if you're prepared to do the work, it can be wonderful.

AREN'T OUR CHILDHOOD LOVES OFTEN THE FIRST THING WE TURN TO?

And Andrea offered some trend spotting, as well; she finds that she's being asked to make comfort food for more and more weddings—baked macaroni and cheese, fried chicken; one bride and groom wanted grilled cheese sandwiches. Andrea made them with manchego and cheddar, sliced them into narrow lengths and served them very hot as appetizers—delicious.

This movement toward the reassuring, the comforting and the homemade sparked something else I'd been thinking about. If my theory that the One-of-a-Kind Wedding Cake started many of us believing that weddings might become more personal, I've also spotted a new trend in many of the weddings we've talked

about for this book: cupcakes. Cupcakes kept popping up in interviews even when the weddings we were discussing weren't all that inventive. When we give ourselves permission to indulge, aren't our childhood loves often the first thing we turn to? I also suspect that if *New American Weddings* is about celebrating the people we really are, then the idea of putting on airs or trying to impress with a reception and food that is not, in fact, what we'd choose to eat if it was our own last meal is proving less appealing. Pounded veal and truffle-laced risottos, precious little beggars' purses filled with caviar and sorbets of rare sauterne may be a wonderful treat, but unless you're the Duchess of Whatsis, they're unlikely to be the food you feel best expresses your own personal style.

Ann Warren owns the Cupcake Café in New York. Like Clare Henry's Glasgow cake-artist, Ann began her professional life as a painter and one can easily see the painterly approach she takes to her butter cream in her garden of cakes.

Ann believes that the Wedding Cupcake had

really taken off after a mention in Martha Stewart's *Wedding* magazine. She often doesn't know the details of the rest of the wedding, but she doesn't seem to think that the cupcake weddings have necessarily tended to be very different from the traditional wedding cake weddings in any respect other than cupcakes.

The cupcake symbolizes a defined trend in wedding receptions, a move to the idea of simple pleasures. A related change appears in Ann's grown-up-size wedding cakes. They look like gems that might have emerged from the kitchen

of a very, very talented mother. Her cake itself is denser, more homey and simple; her butter cream is rich and all is edible and the word "honest" springs to mind in full size or cup.

And a footnote on cakes: Alison Miller, one of our Unitarian ministers, tells about a wedding that seemed traditional in all respects, until the cake appeared—which was made of Rice Krispies and marshmallow. There is a fault line between self-expression and tradition; the first place you are likely to see the break seems to be the cake.

this page:

examples of Ann Warren's cakes

opposite page:

Cupcake Café's Ann Warren

offers cupcakes

FROM CONGA LINES TO PONY RIDES, THE WHOLE POINT IS TO MAKE YOUR GUESTS FEEL THAT YOUR HAPPINESS INVOLVES THEM.

this page:

traditional Irish dancers

entertain at the

Gallahue-Takahashi

reception

opposite page:

scenes from the

McSpadden-Todd reception

Fiona Gallahue and Retsu Takahashi's wedding ceremony celebrated their cultures and backgrounds. As many of Retsu's Japanese family traveled to America for the celebration, Fiona took the opportunity to share her family's Celtic heritage and treat them to traditional Irish music and dance.

The wedding reception is a wonderful place to feature the kind of entertainment you both enjoy. It brings with it a kind of challenge

to invent activities that might engage the largest number of your guests. In our case, we had apple bobbing, sack races and country fair events. Rick Todd's sister, Kate, devised a clever game to be played by the newlyweds, who pro-vided answers to her questions on paddles. There is no right or wrong. From conga lines to pony rides, the whole point is to let your guests feel that your happiness includes them and their delight is yours.

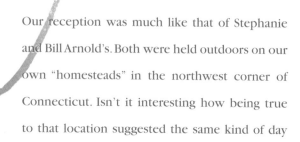

Our reception was much like that of Stephanie and Bill Arnold's. Both were held outdoors on our own "homesteads" in the northwest corner of Connecticut. Isn't it interesting how being true to that location suggested the same kind of day and the same kind of atmosphere? We both wanted country music and country food, a day of ease and fun and we wanted time for children and families to run about and play without worrying about "good behavior."

this page and opposite:

sack races, pony rides,

traditional music, sunflowers,

stalks of corn and hay bales

all go into a down-home

Connecticut-country

wedding reception

MEIER DELANEY
THE WEDDING BARN MENU

I hoped for a country fair where we might present to Frank and his European and English friends the foods we thought best represented America. Andrea Giardino planned the menu:

Bread'n'Butter
Navaho Cornbread, San Francisco
& Sourdough Southern Biscuits
with
Fresh Churned Butter
Ham
Peach Compote
Farmhouse Cheddar
Apples, Pears and Watermelons

Buffalo Grill Won't You Come Out Tonight
Buffalo Burgers on Johnny Cakes or Potato Flour Buns
Corn and Pepper Relish
Local Smokehouse Bacon
Grilled Corn on the Cob
Grilled Beets
Grilled Slices of Vidalia Onions

Out of the Frying Pan and into the Fire
Fried Chicken
Parsnip Fritters
French Fries

Sea Biscuits

Crab Cakes

Maine Lobster Rolls

New England Clam Chowder

Steamed Clams

Pig Roast

(Need we say "More"?)

BBQ and Adobo Sauce

Macaroni and Cheese

The Green Thumb

Wild Rice with Blueberries and Morels

Indian Cress Salad

Heirloom Tomatoes with Wild Fennel

Fresh Vegetable Succotash

Dogwood Cocktail

Lemonade with Blenheim's Spicy Ginger Ale,

with/without Vodka

served in chilled enameled tin mugs

Andrea created an overview of the event and drew her plan for traffic flow to the food stands. We bought enameled tin plates and mugs from a company that makes gear for camping. The long dining tables in the tent were draped with burlap and topped with gingham runners, buckets of sunflowers and bright dahlias. The napkins were bandannas of aqua, yellow, brown and orange, tied in rough bows of hemp.

A Portosan, delivered and parked in the field, offered two washrooms, with toilets, sinks and makeup lighting. Zeze decorated each of them to a fare-thee-well with flowers and farm accessories. One would have thought that the bathrooms from Versailles had been delivered,

this page and opposite:

a country fair atmosphere

was created by offering

activities for all

given the guest response. And while it makes us smile to remember them, it reminds us that while there is nothing romantic about it, bathrooms are one more thing you must think about when planning a reception. They are part of the nuts and bolts that must be tightened right up and looked after, if all is not to come apart under pressure.

The event was laid out like a boulevard around the tent. Zeze, the renowned New York florist, created food stations by laying boards on stacks of hay and decorated the surfaces with vintage tablecloths, pails of flowers, bowls and buckets of apples and delectable offerings of food with individual menus on each table.

THE EVENT
WAS LAID OUT
LIKE A
BOULEVARD
AROUND THE
TENT.

One of Andrea's biggest issues—besides the quality of her food and the creativity of her thinking—is that she believes buffets shouldn't be as difficult or as irritating for guests as they most often are. She is aligned with the idea that guests should feel entertaining is being staged to treat them to something very special. To this end, we usually create food stations, where a variety of different options are served. We've done this at all of our big parties and it's worked wonderfully. Lines rarely form; if there are more than two people in front of you waiting for a lobster roll, go to the next station and pick up a sandwich of barbecued pork from a pig smoked on a spit. Or head over to the gumbo, or the clam chowder, or the bison burgers, or the fried chicken, or the little cones of french fried sweet potatoes, or the baked ham, cornbread and beefsteak tomatoes.

Our wedding cake was our favorite cake of chocolate and orange mousse with ladyfingers, reproduced twenty or thirty times by Belgique, a world-class patisserie that happened to have landed (we imagined like a shipwrecked aristocrat) in tiny Kent, Connecticut.

Dixie Todd joined Andrea in the coordination of our reception and provided the staff, who wore white shirts, khaki pants and aprons stamped with our signature D logo in different sizes and colors.

For all their good intentions, can solid, clever, talented professionals ensure that your whole event will seem just as easy as pie? Not on your life.

Can they make it easier, warmer, run more smoothly, taste better, delight your guests and eliminate (or deal with) some of the more unpleasant surprises every event engenders? They certainly can.

Your job: Find planners and caterers who endorse your idea of a New American Wedding. You don't need one more person on your team to read you "the rules" when they're not what you want. You don't need a baker to tell you that you can't have a banana walnut wedding cake. You don't need a wedding coordinator to tell you that you need a bride's side and a groom's side of an aisle when your friends love you both. You don't need one more person to raise an eyebrow when you are trying for all you're worth, to make a day that's unique and all about you. I found those people and I've shared with you how they helped me. You now have a benchmark to judge others against.

So on the fourteenth of September in 2002, amid potato sack races and horseshoe throws,

Frank and I married, celebrated, and 150 friends and neighbors shared the day with us. They danced the two-step and listened to Dixieland, sang along with a barbershop quartet and ate fried chicken, buffalo burgers and parsnip fritters. Most of all, they applauded our promise to love, honor and support one another, and to stand together first as we deal with the problems and the challenges handed our way by life.

Somehow at a wedding celebration, there exists in the air the idea of blue skies forever. The whole reception is staged to suggest that it will be so. But the reality is, in its way, even better. Life will test you, there's no getting around it; and it probably already has. But from here on in there is someone in your corner and the slings and arrows they talk about will be buffered by two. There is someone there, standing, as Frank says, "on your square"—to perceive that you're hurt, comfort if you're glum, rejoice when you're delighted, applaud when you succeed. And if that's not a better reason for celebration than blue skies, I don't know what is.

CHAPTER 10

THE HONEYMOON

ANNE WATKINS AND DAVID MILLMAN MARRIED AT HOME
IN A CEREMONY AND RECEPTION DESIGNED TO BE SMALL
ENOUGH AND HOME COOKED ENOUGH TO ALLOW THEM
THE CHANCE TO BLOW THEIR BUDGET ON A GREAT
VENETIAN HONEYMOON.

They compacted all their joy into one Riverside Drive apartment and the judge who married them sliced the roast.

Anne and David then took a break from their professional tasks as painter and photographer, respectively, and set out for Venice, where they stayed in the apartment of a gallery owner from Manhattan. They took long walks, lunched in the cafés and piazzas, tracked and backtracked the tiny curving streets that revealed wonders at every turn. Most important, they did what artists do—they took in the sights and, with their own

natural gifts, held them forever in their art.

Nothing points out the opportunities of a honeymoon better than this Honeymoon Portfolio of Anne and David's time together in Venice. All art is, after all, communication. Writing, painting, photography, music—all create the opportunity to see and feel something through another's eyes. Art opens a world to another person. It tells you what of the world impressed them and how they felt about it. It lets you consider another point of view. Honeymoons allow that same opportunity of reflection and insight,

this chapter:

paintings of Venice by Anne and

photographs by David, taken on

their honeymoon

without distractions or tugs from the rest of the world. And if we, personally, have fewer or lesser talents than David and Anne, our passions and our convictions, our grasp of the world around us, our values and our delights might still be filtered and shared through someone else, and their life will be richer for it. Naturally, the converse is true as well and we see and grow and learn through them.

Sarah Morris and Jeffrey Michael planned a honeymoon road trip across America while Sara Hudson and Ron Gold relaxed in Florida. Frank and I tried to create an iconic Hollywood-style honeymoon and drove to Niagara, and while we found that like Oscar Wilde, we would have been more impressed had the falls run upstream, the drive to Canada and back was filled with talk and

what we like to call downloading. Time alone, after all, is the thing you're looking for, not the creation of one more stressful, impressive event.

Weddings are exhausting. It's not just the preparation and the organization that can wear you out; they are, almost by nature, fraught with emotion. Most of it good, it must be said, but don't be deluded into thinking that you will just sail

through this experience; down the road lies an ambush.

The older you are, the more of life you bring with you and the very things this day will celebrate—your children, families, businesses, responsibilities—will be on your mind. The kindest and most generous people in your life will warmly accept and joyfully relish your choices simply because they are yours. But we all care for people—be they family, friends or professional associates—who need more care than others, for all kinds of legitimate and not-so-legitimate reasons. And, in a way, that's a big part of what this day is meant to commemorate; your troubles are

now shared and doubled; full and personal and real.

Consider seriously a honeymoon getaway of some kind—even a few days, where the two of you can download the glory of the day you planned so well and relax without the stress of

family, caterers and Portosan pickups, calls from your offices or other people's needs. It needn't be grand or fancy. Call it a break or a wedding trip; call it a honeymoon, call it a good idea. The challenges and opportunities of real life will be waiting for you soon enough.

CHAPTER 11

ALL THE KING'S MEN

THERE ARE MANY REASONS WHY COUPLES FALL BACK ON TRADITION AT THE EXPENSE OF THE INDIVIDUALS THEY'VE BEEN SET TO CELEBRATE. EVEN WHEN THESE RITES AND RITUALS DON'T FIT THE COUPLE, CREATING THINGS AFRESH IS HARD WORK.

*I*f this book has done anything for you, I hope it's been to suggest that the work is worth it. That by celebrating the truth of the two of you, there is a greater sense of connection with the ritual itself, a greater understanding of your commitment within your community and a deeper idea of your promise and meaning to each other. But have I said anywhere that it's easy? I hope not.

I also hope that I've said clearly and enough times to be heard that you will need help. You need help in the planning and help in the execution, and while it may be from friends, some part, or all of it will need the eye, the experience, the skill and the smarts of professionals.

That said, you must understand that all professionals are not created equal. The first cut will need to come by clearly evaluating whether or not the planner, caterer, photographer, graphic designer, jeweler, dressmaker, florist or personal shopper truly understands that you don't want an Old Traditional Wedding. That you really want to create something new and all about you has to be the theme

of your first conversation. And you need to listen for the hints that might tell you that though they are smiling and nodding, they're not in it for the long haul. If they give you answers like "All of our brides . . . " or "This is how I handle . . . ," begin to edge away from their desk.

It's important, too, to recognize that this is a business for professionals. One of the ways they have been able to make it a profitable business is by repeating the same kinds of things over and over again. They don't have a learning curve; they just have another girl in another white dress. I'm the last one to suggest that professionals shouldn't be fairly paid. So don't be rude, don't even be disappointed, just move on. While it's tempting to hope that the town's most highly regarded caterer (or planner or designer) will come around to your way of thinking, don't fall into the trap of believing that you will be able to teach an old dog new tricks. These are their tricks and they like them; they've made their reputations on them and they mean to repeat them.

Somewhere, probably within earshot, there is someone of talent, skill, empathy and guts who wants to create something new; you just have to find them. And, by the way, don't assume that the town's most status-worthy professional isn't interested in creating something new; he or she might have been waiting for just the right client. And you might be the breath of fresh air they've been hoping for!

Interview them early in the process, before you have all of your ideas in line. Look at their previous work and see how their taste aligns with yours. Listen carefully to their answers to your questions. Do you sense that they understand you? Do not expect to see your wedding in their pictures or workbook. If you did, it wouldn't be new. You want to understand their thinking and their creativity and their taste. See which of them adds to the process and go with those who have the greatest degree of interest in discovering ways to celebrate your unique spirit. They'll be in it for their own reasons, creative and fulfilling—and because they'll like the idea of moving the culture along with original ideas. When everyone involved feels that they get something wonderful and beyond payment by being involved in a project, it's bound to be a success. Look for that creative spirit.

WHEN EVERYONE INVOLVED FEELS THAT THEY GET SOMETHING WONDERFUL.

We've talked about dresses, receptions and food and I've introduced you to a number of artists and vendors whom I've found who set a kind of benchmark for this new type of celebration. Share these stories and open up the conversation with your own vendors. Here are a few ways of working that I've learned from my commercial work, but which hold very true for your job as the monarchs of this little fiefdom that will be your wedding.

Keep everyone informed.

There will be times, regardless of how simple, approachable or comfortable you expect your celebration to be, when you will feel like Field Marshal Montgomery out there surveying the troops. On a project that breaks new ground, everyone should be filled in on the concept, the look, the manner and the positioning of the event.

Create visual context.

It's a great idea to make up a sheet or two of references—visuals and some text. In our business we call them reference boards or image boards. You may not be able to describe the dress you want but you may find a picture of a vintage tablecloth that has the feel of what you are thinking of. Cut it out and paste it on the board. Maybe you'll find a picture of a room in France where the carpet is made of the blue and white awning stripes you've been hoping to find in a bridesmaid's dress. Maybe the typography in a headline on an ad for wine will have

the feeling you're hoping to create in an invitation. Perhaps you can find a quote that sums up what you want to say with your celebration. From "Home is where the heart is" to "Life is a banquet"—you have a whole world of books and movies at your feet.

Discuss and evaluate everything with your partner.

Share these boards of color and thinking with each other. Talk them through. Once it's in a form that's manageable—be it a single sheet or a full notebook—go back for one last look and make sure that it is focused. As you debate and test each other, you'll find yourselves coming to deeper truths and a clearer idea about what it is you stand for when you stand together. We all long to hear what it is you two want to say.

Trust your suppliers.

You don't have to know how to accomplish the thing—that's what you will share with your

planner or your caterer or your dressmaker. You don't have to do (in fact you shouldn't do) their job, but you have to give them the tools to do their job in the best possible way, on your behalf. Give them all the same full treatment. Assume the florist needs the same background the caterer needs. Everything that goes into the whole should be shared with the team. And then set them free to come up with their own creative ideas.

This is exactly the process I use when lining up professionals to use in my work in marketing, advertising, graphics or events. I create a team and everyone from the producer to the fashion stylist, from the photographer to the hair and makeup artist, from the calligrapher to the printer sees and hears the same inspirational themes. Don't assume that anyone's job is too small or too separate.

Bring everyone together.

At some point, once your team has been chosen, you should plan a meeting to bring them all together at the site. For some reason, this can be the most difficult thing to accomplish. Everyone has a pressured schedule. No one ever wants to meet the other team members, and I don't know why, because these gatherings often turn out to be wonderful.

This said, your job will be in creating a meeting that is very respectful of your vendors' time. Don't make the caterer sit for two hours while you discuss flowers. Don't allow the planner to go off with the man who will rent the tables, when everyone needs to decide how the room should be oriented and whether to use long narrow tables or lots of rounds. These things involve the caterer and the florist/room dresser and the planner in all kinds of ways and their work together (or apart) could create very big differences in effect. You need to manage their working cooperatively together.

Beyond what we've already touched upon through the book, here are some of the outside talents you may use to pull your wedding into focus.

The McSpadden-Todd Colorado Wedding

A hasty person misses the
sweet things.
- Swahili proverb

Trip Recommendations

Travel Dates: I recommend flying in Friday morning and taking the scenic drive Vail. The scenic drive involves taking Highway 6 instead of the Interstate where possible. For a MapQwest map click here.

I recommend staying through SundayJuly 4th and flying out on Monday. The Vail and Avon fireworks are amazing and worth the extra day in town. You could also use the day to see the area.

Dining:

Sweet Basil is our favorite and also Kate Todd's (Rick's sister). You MUST get the hot sticky toffee for dessert.

Game Creek restaurant is an experience. After riding Vail's gondola you will be taken by shuttle to the restaurant. Has to be seen to be believed.

Narayan's Nepalese When Narayan's opened in 1990 in Boulder, it was one of only three Nepalese restaurants in the United States. A year later, Narayan's was named as one of the top three vegetarian restaurants in America by the Vegetarian Journal. It has since moved to Avon, CO, and also has opened a Thai restaurant.

La Cantina Is consistently voted the best Mexican food in the Vail Valley. The location seems strange - the main Vail parking structure, but the food and margaritas more than make up for environment. A great place for a cheap lunch.

Make The Most Of Your Visit:

- If you have any questions or concerns about what to do with your free time, email rick@rickanddiana.com , or contact the Vail Recreation District .

Invitations

The first hint of the style of a wedding is, inevitably, the invitation. Younger new American couples have taken to the idea of e-mail invites in a way that takes my breath away, so fast is the cultural change. They can add photographs, illustrations, links to bridal registries, maps and directions, lists and numbers for hotels and accommodations, notes, a guest list with e-mail addresses, so that transportation might be shared. It turns out to be so efficient and so easily personalized that I fear the art of ink on paper could be justifiably endangered.

Still, there is nothing to equal an invitation so beautifully designed or exquisitely produced that the whole idea of the wedding becomes tantalizingly apparent as a don't-miss affair. Here are a few we love (and a couple we've done).

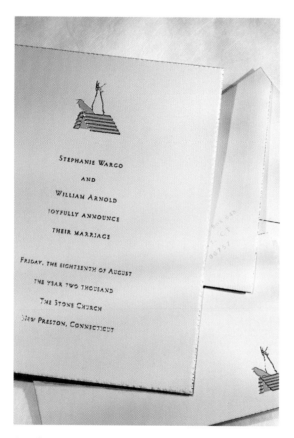

Stephanie Wargo's invitation to her own wedding contained the image of a tiny bird that actually sat at the edge of their barn on its birdhouse, guarding its mate. Stephanie is a brilliant creator of custom-designed invitations making use of engraving, embossing, letter press printing, and beautiful papers.

Retsu Takahashi designed a graphic, modern invitation that uses the calligraphic mark of the Japanese "and" as its ampersand. The colorful map acts as an endpaper that is also completely functional.

The marriage of Joyce Castleberry and Gerry Hovagimyan confirmed the commitment of a couple who had already created a life together, full of art and craft. Gerry is an artist whose work is always on the edge of breakthrough technologies. Joyce is a classicist. To create an invitation for them, I chose a deliberate art-based form, rather midcentury in feel, to suggest the classic nature of the Modern and the New.

Our own invitation was casual, graphic, witty, pretty and full of words that read like a story. I designed it in a mix of papers and tied it up with a gingham bow. It allowed me to present the colors and feeling of the day to our guests, giving a hint of what they would find at the wedding.

Food

There will be all kinds of food decisions—seated or buffet, passed food, open bar, only champagne, food before, food after or constant food. When push comes to shove, I believe that the thing to remember here is that you want to wow your audience with how delicious the food is and how clever you are.

You don't want quantity over quality and you don't want quantity over budget. There are wonderful food opportunities to be had at every possible price range. You might choose omelet stations, allowing every possible kind of filling, and dessert stations with a make-your-own-sundae options that are greater and more indulgent than a childhood memory (none of this is break the bank stuff, by the way). Or a full, truffles-flown-in-from-the-Perigord-this-morning-six-course sit-down meal with a waiter behind every chair.

If you are wearing an Irish linen pinafore and pale pink linen ballet slippers, carrying lilacs, with your hair tied up in a grosgrain bow, the lunch of omelets would be a perfect choice. So,

did you get there by way of the budget or the look and feel of the event? But you must understand, the budget is a huge part of the look and feel of the event.

The way you want to present yourself is about the truth of your lives, not the fantasy that you are somehow, this night, the Duke and Duchess of Tiptoe. If Irish linen and eggs are what you can afford, do it beautifully and do it with great style. Don't let a caterer talk you into anything that is fancier, more involved or more expensive than you want or need.

One other hint: Unless there is a very particular cake you have your heart set on from the first, coordinate your cake with your caterer and planner. While I was amused by the idea of the Rice Krispie cake mentioned earlier in the book, I think it makes no sense in a completely traditional wedding. I feel there should have been some hint of playfulness that made the cake a more cohesive part of the meal and the whole event. You may be forgiven if you lose focus when you see or hear something that fires your

imagination, but your caterer/planner should be counted on to keep those kinds of details (and you) in line.

Flowers

Flowers can be just that, flowers—your bouquet and a boutonniere for your groom. Or it can be a floral designer who can manage the transformation of a site—like turning an empty barn into a space bedecked and dressed for a turn-of-the-last-century saloon dance or a tent into an Indian palace or your living room into a garden.

The best floral designers, Robert Isabell, Preston Bailey, Zeze, have one thing in common—they can make things appear where nothing existed before. They are magicians—set designers for the theater of life.

They create weddings and parties all over the world, and often, for their clients, price is no object. But they are real pros, and I promise you,

THEY ARE MAGICIANS— SET DESIGNERS FOR THE THEATER OF LIFE.

they can also turn out brilliant work within a reasonable budget. Is it your budget? How can I know. But in your town, there may be the talent and the style to accomplish just what you need, if you ask and inform and guide and inspire in the right way.

Whether it's Zeze or your local find, they'll need colors and themes and access to your planner and/or caterer. Together you will decide how you want to dress the rooms you will use for your ceremony and your reception. Make them an important part of the conversations you have toward this event.

Floral designers are also a wonderful source of props. In my case: old wheelbarrows they filled with tall flowers, a grand old tractor cart, rusting watering cans, mellow baskets, ancient wicker suitcases, tin luminaries with star cutouts to show the flicker of candles; they delivered cartons of old Ball jars, whiskey jugs, colored sap buckets and tin cans to hold bouquets on tables, and an old farm ladder supported pots of flowers on its rungs.

Whoever you get to rent or coordinate the table settings, make sure they work hand in hand with the floral designer and, if you've chosen your professionals right, you'll get the most glorious results.

Music

Almost nothing is more difficult, I think. I am not a fan of wedding bands and I suppose by this time, you know me well enough to not be surprised by this news. The band that breaks into "Celebration time—all right!" would not be playing at my wedding. But this is your wedding, not mine. You really have to think about the mood and the experience you want to share. If you want to dance that chicken dance, or the macarena, or the alley cat (am I dating myself?), by all means, go to it. But take the time to think through exactly what you do want and understand that the music can set the tone of your wedding as much as anything else you might do. It can bring people together, teach them

new things and create a soundtrack by which people will think of you as a couple.

I love music that is simply there to be enjoyed. Chamber groups, string quartets, jazz combos, new world groups, acoustic, traditional—like a fiddle and a mandolin—and I love cocktail piano. I love dance music—great Motown; real, authentic rock 'n' roll; big band, Vienna waltzes with a lush orchestra; bluegrass and country; Irish traditional music; even German polka bands. But I like them real and not ersatz. Trust me, music will do a wonderful job of setting the mood you hope to convey.

Do you want your crowd up on their feet? Think about how it works with the style of the event you are hoping to create or achieve. No one says (at least not in *this* book) that you must have dancing at a wedding (at least not at *your* wedding). So, once again, *you* decide. I interviewed a couple who wanted more than anything to tango, and for the year leading up to their wedding they went to tango classes. The band they hired was chosen because of their tangos, and all through

the night, they tangoed to the complete delight of their guests. Consider a square dance complete with caller, or a teacher for two-stepping, Morris dancing, cha-chas or Lindy. People are brought together by shared experience and music and dance can be the perfect tools.

Photography

Recording your Wedding Ahh. Maybe my favorite part of this exercise. Because the visual arts is the world I come from, this is where I get to make the point that these professionals, all of them are, each in his or her way, artists. They are not machines and they are not commodities. You won't get the same dress from any two designers—if either is any good. And you won't get the same meal or the same flowers, if you've followed our thinking. A great caterer is no less an artist than a jewelry designer.

But the thing you will hold in your hand, long after the wedding, the thing that will help you remember the day are the photographs. Let me take you through some of my favorite photographers and you will see distinct differences in their work and their style. This should help you in your own search to train your eye and your thinking to evaluate and choose the way you want your wedding to be recorded.

John Dolan

John Dolan took the pictures of the York-Bogen masquerade ball as well as the pictures of Anne Watkins and David Millman. And while they are very different, you can see an art photography sensibility in his work, a feeling for movement and mystery and a fearlessness about capturing time.

He works for the most part with available light, although, in my opinion, his pictures for Nic York and Matt Bogen were enhanced by the otherworldliness of his flash. He learned from the photographer Sylvia Plachy, whose art has put her in the forefront of modern collectible photographers. In fact, John tells us that Sylvia photographed his own wedding, and for eight hours, out of the corner of his eye, he could see her make choices about what was important and what was beautiful. He felt her lean into a moment and reinforce his instinct that the moment was, in fact, as significant as he felt it might be. To this day he says that he thinks of this each time he photographs a wedding.

John Dolan

180 Varick Street

New York, NY 10014

212.462.2598

www.johndolan.com

John tells us that the best clients arrange to meet their photographers in advance, review their work and look to find a common way of seeing life. He reminds us that you are going to be with a photographer in a very intimate setting for hours, on one of the most exposed and emotionally open days of your life. "You better like him," warns John. You also better like his or her work.

You need to tell a photographer what you hope to have him accomplish in photographing your wedding. Do you want to make sure you get a picture with your father or your dog? But we should warn you, a long list of "must have" photographs is not going to get you wonderful results.

My suggestion: If you want to make sure you have pictures of each of your guests, consider a portrait studio setup, as I had, in addition to the reportage of your wedding. More about that? Read on.

John is a true romantic. At some point in the middle of the reception, he takes the bride and groom out of the fray, away from the

crowd, and allows them to decompress and talk about their feelings. Some of his most touching pictures come from these moments. His photographs clearly illustrate how he feels about love and family—his own as well as yours. This is the kind of intellectual and emotional connection you should be looking for with your own photographer, if you want pictures that are beautiful and full of affection and warmth.

Lynne Brubaker

Lynne Brubaker

434.296.9376

lynne@brubakerphoto.com

www.lynnebrubaker.com

Lynne began her professional life as a model and she brings her fashion eye to her work covering weddings. Time of day is critical to her as she shoots exclusively (or as exclusively as possible) with natural, available light—so weddings after dark, she'll tell you right up front, are not for her. This is an important lesson to note: Don't fall in love with a photographer's work and then ask her to shoot something completely outside of her style or voice.

And Lynne offers a tip to you on the issue of nighttime weddings: If you have invested in a fabulous setting, do try to get the most out of it. Too many weddings, she feels, begin at sunset and the darkness of night all but obliterates the spectacular views, gardens or architectural details.

She sees herself as telling "the story of the wedding" and finds that too many formal family portraits keep her from doing just that. Even her family photos feel casual and loose, but with a fashionable sensibility that has a bit of commercial polish to them. Lynne photographed the McSpadden–Todd wedding in this book, and I think you can clearly see the even-handed storytelling grace she was able to bring to this shoot.

Lynne also suggests that to get the best results, the bride and groom should plan ahead and organize their time during the wedding day to devote to the art of photography, coordinating this with their photographer to get the most out of the best light of the day. They should assemble and supervise their wedding party to accommodate the limits of time and nature. "Better," Lynne warns, "to allot extra time, in case someone gets lost or has to be hunted down."

Clearly advice from a pro who has seen it all.

If the wedding is very large or high profile, or if the logistics are difficult, Lynne may suggest doubling up on photographers. This is a great hint and can give you a lot to think about in evaluating what you hope to capture from your day.

In light of Lynne's note, Frank and I were clear about the fact that we did, in fact, want pictures of everyone else for our wedding album. We come to this from completely different positions. Frank had his own television and radio programs in England, and he thinks of his image as a part of his commercial wares. I have spent most of my life on the other side of the set and find I'm a fish out of water in front of a camera.

At any rate, Roxanne Lowit was there, like the dear friend she is, to make us feel as comfortable as possible, and we arranged for the smartest part of our celebration in our concept of the Photo-Studio-in-the Field.

Roxanne Lowit

Roxanne Lowit

212.244.6466

roxannelowit@aol.com

www.roxannelowit.com

One of New York's top fashion and event reportage photographers, Roxanne has taken pictures that grace *Vanity Fair, European Vogue* and *Harper's Bazaar* as well as the ads in *Cosmopolitan*. Tony publisher Assouline has published books of her edgy celebrity and fashion photographs.

Her wedding work is usually directed to rock stars and fashion folk, for good reason: Roxanne's superb, witty, iconoclastic eye catches the Weegee moment with a high degree of style. Although she covered our soft-focus country wedding so sensitively and beautifully, her real métier is in the urban and the chic. Rox is flown all over the world to cover parties and weddings in her very unique and individualistic photographic voice. If you want your wedding to look like a glamorous celebrity happening, this is the kind of photography you might choose.

Peter Hamblin

Peter set up the outdoor studio as a fully lit set, complete with backdrop, bales of hay and props of pitchforks, shovels, pails, whiskey jugs, straw hats, cowboy hats and bouquets of flowers.

His background as a photographer who has combined work on weddings with more staid, controlled-light corporate photography and portraiture made him the perfect choice for this role. On top of this, he is unflappable, managing to ease and comfort even the most prickly subject. As one who has had to get in and out of a CEO's office with a portrait in less time than it takes to tie a shoelace, we felt sure he could manage our herd of friends and loved ones in groups, pairs, families and even on their own. Peter travels to events and corporations wherever planes, trains and cars are free to go, but if you are looking for local talent to set up an on-site studio, try to find someone who is familiar with taking formal, beautifully lit portraits of nonprofessionals. Personality is as important as skill here because you will want your guests to feel at ease and look their best.

Pete's mentor, and the photographer whose work has graced more of our ads than any other, Ken Skalski, helped him set up a system linked to a computer and printer. Portraits were printed in sepia, put in frames and given to all guests as their favor, right on the spot. It was completely brilliant.

Peter Hamblin

719. 351. 5983

Ken Skalski

MEIER

www.meierbrand.com

212. 460. 5655

If you can afford the doubling up of photographers to cover reportage and portraits, I think you get the best of both worlds with this unorthodox approach—an artistically personalized idea of the nature and flow of your wedding paired with a study of each of your guests, as a documentary of this special day in your shared lives.

You will avoid the inevitable string of photographs of relatives and friends with their mouths open and their eyes closed. You will avoid the shots around tables with half-eaten meals in full view. You will avoid taking an art photographer and forcing him or her to succumb to mind-numbing shots of "the bride with Aunt Emma," neither getting the best of his efforts nor the best of Aunt Emma.

Anne Watkins

227 Riverside Drive

New York, NY 10025

212.866.0057

anne@annewatkins.com

Anne Watkins

There is one other approach I heartily endorse: the surprising idea of the "Painted Wedding." Had I known that Anne Watkins existed in time for my own wedding, she would surely have been part of the mix. Anne does the impossible—she captures the wedding day in watercolor. Highly impressionistic, these little works of art are created on the spot and become part of a family's legacy and heirlooms. She tells us that she feels she is almost invisible, quietly taking in the scenes around her. Often guests tell her that they weren't even aware of her presence, sitting on the sidelines, painting away—although some ask for a special little proof in paint of their being at the scene. She is at the least a benign and gentle presence and not a timbre of thunder is stolen from the couple as the gallery watches her work. She picks her weddings carefully and is, as are all of the artists featured here, flown to weddings around the world, to capture moments on paper in ways that will certainly color the way couples remember the day they chose to say "I do."

One last note about video recording the wedding. At the risk of seeming a curmudgeon, it is neither a form of documentation nor a presence I particularly like. Perhaps it is because I've spent so much of my time on commercial sets that the presence of the camera and crew feels more like work. Though the equipment and the crews have gotten smaller through the years, there remains, at least for me, a kind of invasion of a personal event that doesn't exist with a still camera. As a last note, I don't know a bride or groom who has looked at his or her

wedding videos more than a few times while a few beautiful images from a wedding are almost always framed and placed on a desk, a dresser or a piano to remind you and friends and family of that treasured day, or to share with visitors and introduce them to the more personal and intimate part of your life.

Regardless of how you manage it, from providing disposable cameras to all of your guests to renting a photo booth to bringing an artist into your family, make sure you give proper attention to holding on to the images of this day and the

community of friends and family who will gather around you.

Your wedding is going to be made up of many people, from those who will share it to the many who will help you control, accomplish and fulfill your dream of a day, as perfect as you can make it. As John Dolan suggested, it is important to like the artists who will become your vendors, suppliers and team members. Indeed, perhaps it is more important in a New American Wedding than in a traditional event, because you are going to set off on a road of discovery about your val-

ues and your sense of style, your ideas of appropriateness, family, privacy, generosity, money, fashion, history, comfort and love. At the end of the journey, you'll have created an event that speaks for and about the two of you. Your fellow travelers can enhance and support your vision, but they should not, and cannot, create it.

This wedding is all about you; it is a New American Wedding and, in a way, anything goes— as long as it goes your way.

CONTRIBUTORS

Rosemary and Allison gave of their time and shared their thoughtful, well-intended and hard-won wisdom.

Rev. Rosemary Bray McNatt
The 4th Universalist Society
160 Central Park West
New York, NY
212.595.1658

Rosemary's spectacular personality and progressive vision make her a great choice for any marriage, but she seems to find special connection with couples of mixed race and has managed to calm the path of many family issues.

Rev. Alison Miller
All Souls Unitarian Church
1157 Lexington Avenue
New York, NY 10021
212.535.5530

Alison is a Harvard Divinity graduate and the product of a Jewish and a Christian parent. She has grace, wit and personal insight into the issues of mixed culture marriages.

As a note: All Souls has a lovely church, a very pretty small chapel and one of New York's great music directors with a team of ministers who are all top notch

CATERERS, FLORISTS, PARTY PLANNERS

I asked for stories and recipes, checked facts, ran ideas, laughed and cried and laughed some more. These names prove, once more, that creativity so often goes hand in hand with a generous spirit.

Andrea Giardino
Giardino Enterprises
212.595.5654

For more than a decade I've trusted Andrea to create the most spectacular food and parties for my business (and what little there is in our life that is not business). She can do the little gorgeous canapés you see all over town, but I think she's best with real food. The kind of things you want to eat, not look at.

Andrea is an inside secret and most of her clients would not be comfortable being mentioned—but I will tell you that she's done events for New York's most important fashion/retail family, heads of state, movie stars and cultural icons. And she always manages to serve up wit and grace and creativity. We were told recently by one of her brilliant captains that her freelance staff, many of whom are also registered with the best caterers in town, would hold their dates for a chance to work with Andrea. "It's a superior gig," she explained. "Everything about it is a cut above; the intelligence, the planning, the food and the fun." I may be prejudiced, but I couldn't have said it better myself.

Zeze
Zeze Flowers
212.753.7767

If you've read this far, you know that Zeze created all the flowers and decoration for our wedding. And he has done the flowers for almost every party I've given for more than twenty years. I'm not alone in thinking that he and his on-the-job-designer-wife, Peggy, are completely wonderful. But if you don't simply want to take my word for it, ask Bette Midler or Sting; or just about anyone in publishing or theater or the highest high society.

It's not just because Zeze is the most creative florist we know—it's also because he mixes a sensibility of light, fresh delight with the grounding classical detail of antiques and topiary, moss-covered urns and nineteenth-century garden seats; old crystal ice buckets and antique maple-sap buckets, Italian pottery and Flemish still-life paintings. His eye for the right prop is unerring. But ask him to create an environment, and he will give you something incredibly beautiful that is also remarkably real. There is a down-to-earth quality in the patina, the choice of objects, the sensitivity of his vision that is, in my opinion, unmatched.

His wonderful new Beekman Place space on First Avenue is available for parties and could be a great venue on its own.

Preston Bailey
Preston Bailey Entertainment and Set Design, Inc.
212.691.6777
prestonbailey.com

Just knowing that Preston created weddings for Matt Lauer, Donald Trump and Melissa Rivers, and parties for Oprah should give you an idea of the quality of his workmanship and the level of his price tag. But for those who want pure fantasy, there may be no one better. His latest book, *Preston Bailey's Fantasy Weddings,* allows everyone an insider's look at the scale of his work and his edge-pushing and theatrical approach to weddings. His website is a real tour through his world.

Robert Isabell
Robert Isabell, Inc.
212.290.2428

Robert's team can plan all aspects of your wedding, except for the food; and he's done just this, for clients as design institutional as MOMA, as celebrity chic as Sarah Jessica Parker, as socially in the know as Caroline Kennedy and Aerin Lauder. Open to talking about all budgets, we know that his studio is another real asset to the Big Concept Event.

My own take is that Robert's strength is his mix of creativity and inventiveness with impeccable taste. Handsome and gifted, he becomes a great friend of his clients and his kindnesses are legend.

PARTY PLANNER

As far as party planners go, I've never used one as a resource separate from a caterer or florist in NYC. But in Connecticut, I wouldn't dream of scheduling so much as a dinner party without calling Anne Perry Todd (known to her friends as Dixie). Her staffing is impeccable, her vendors (tents, Portosans, fireworks, etc.) are tops and her experience is unbeatable.

Anne Perry Todd
Party Resources
860.927.4034

Sylvia Weinstock and Ann Warren gave of their time and their resources so generously to help this book become a reality. But, of course, the real stars are the cakes they produce, somewhere between art and the art of the treat!

Sylvia Weinstock Cakes
212.925.6698
sylviaweinstock.com
She started the trend and she continues to lead. Her work for moguls, movie stars and assorted royal families might suggest that her cakes are not for you, but don't assume anything until you've talked to her. Most of all, rest assured her wedding cakes are not only the most beautiful in town, they are considered the most classically delicious—tender, perfectly balanced and all you would hope they'd be.

Cupcake Café
Ann Warren
212.465.1530
A wonderful, artistic, flower-bowered garden of cakes as well as cupcakes are available at Ann's Cupcake Café, and her latest café in Books of Wonder on West Eighteenth Street. Beneath the bright buttercream is a cake that says "Mom"; dense and rich with homemade texture.

Ann Warren's cakes are a kind of folk art that I think are just wonderful. If Sylvia's cakes are the Ritz in Paris, Ann's are a farmhouse in Kansas. And I mean that in the most marvelous way!

Zoran, Ulla Maija and Ralph Rucci are available at Saks Fifth Avenue, Bergdorf Goodman and Neiman Marcus. They also conduct their couture businesses from their own salons, where they met with me and contributed invaluable insight into the business of weddings and the psychology of women and dress.

Ulla Maija Couture
24 West 40th Street
New York, NY 10018
212.768.0707

CHADO Ralph Rucci
552 Seventh Avenue
New York, NY 10018
212.819.9066

Zoran
212.233.2025.

Saks Fifth Avenue
12 East 49th Street
New York, NY 10022
212.753.4000
To locate a store near you, visit:
www.saksfifthavenue.com

Bergdorf Goodman
754 Fifth Avenue at 58th Street
New York, NY 10019
212.753.7300

Neiman Marcus
To locate a store near you, visit:
www.neimanmarcus.com

Phil LaDuca's shoes can be found in his New York shop but also in a few outlets across the country. Check the website.

LaDuca Shoes
534 9th Avenue
New York, NY 10018
212.268.6751
www.laDucashoes.com

Our panel of jewelers was very helpful in keeping us on track. They are: Phyllis Bergman, president, Mercury Ring Corporation; Geri Bondanza, vice president, Michael Bondanza, Inc.; Marcee Feinberg, VP Marketing, Lazare Kaplan International; Susan Fortgang, vice president, M. Fabrikant & Sons and Rita Scaglione, president, Fusaro Jewelry Co. Our panel was pulled together, cajoled and handheld by Rachel Rosen—I don't think one could find a more respected or admired woman in the jewelry industry.

Rachel Rosin
914.941.2126
As "Consultant to the Jewelry Industry," Rachel takes assignments on behalf of manufacturers and designers. But one of the tasks she likes best is guiding "civilians" through the industry and matching them with the gems and jewelry of their dreams. If you are on such a hunt, give her a call.

The retail jewelers and manufacturers who generously allowed us the chance to shoot their beautiful merchandise for this book:

Tiffany & Co.
Fifth Avenue at 57th Street
New York, NY 10022
212.755.8000
Personal shopping: 888.546.5188
www.Tiffany.com

Harry Winston
718 Fifth Avenue
New York, NY
212.245.2000

James Robinson, Inc.
Joan Boening
480 Park Avenue
New York, NY 10022
212.752.6166

Lyme Regis, Ltd.
Main Street
Kent, CT 06757
860.927.3330

Rita Fusaro
576 Fifth Avenue
New York, NY 10036
212.860.0151
www.Fusaro.com

Michael Bondanza, Inc.
Geri Bondanza
10 West 46th Street
New York, NY 10036
800.835.0041

Stephanie Wargo
860.927.4879
Stephanie Wargo creates custom-designed social stationery—expensive and worth every penny—that is to paper what French couture is to clothing. She'll find a gorgeous way to interpret your event and create excitement long before the day itself.

NEW AMERICAN BRIDES AND GROOMS

All of us at **MEIER** wish to thank the couples who so generously shared their contacts, their notebooks, their wedding albums, their stories, their valuable time and their New American Weddings with us.

Rachel and Ben Rosin

September 17, 1995

Sara Hudson and Ronald Gold

September 19, 1998

David and Debbie Bain

July 2, 1999

Stephanie Wargo and Bill Arnold

August 18, 2000

Ellen Carrucci and Will Tracy

October 27, 2000

Nic York and Matt Bogen

April 7, 2001

Clare Henry and Phillip Bruno

March 2, 2002

Anne Watkins and David Millman

January 5, 2003

Susan Bednar and John Long

May 22, 2004

Diana McSpadden and Rick Todd

July 3, 2004

Fiona Gallahue and
Retsu Takahashi

September 18, 2004

Sarah and Jeffrey Michael

November 6, 2004

PHOTO CREDITS

2: Photography by Roxanne Lowit

3: Courtesy of Frank Delaney

5: All photography by Ken Skalksi

6: Photography by Peter Hamblin

7: Laurie Gaboardi for *The Litchfield County Times*

9: All images courtesy of Diane Meier Delaney

11: Photography by Peter Hamblin

18: Photography by Carlo Giorgi for Mr. and Mrs. John Long

19: Courtesy of Mr. and Mrs. C.P. Dennehy

35: Photography by John P. Dolan

38: © Genevieve Naylor / CORBIS

39: Photography by Ken Skalksi

40: Photography by Ken Skalksi

41: Courtesy of Mr. and Mrs. Ben Rosin

42: Photography by Pamela Duffy

43-58: Photography by Ken Skalksi

60: © Comstock Images / Getty Images

62: Photography by Carlo Giorgi for Mr. andMrs. John Long

63: From top left clockwise: photography by Tom Rosenthal; photography by Pamela Duffy; photography by Carlo Giorgi for Mr. and Mrs. John Long; photography by John Dolan

65: All pictures courtesy of Mr. and Mrs. John Long

70: Courtesy of "Wolfe" Range

74: Photography by Tom Rosenthal

78: Photography by Roxanne Lowit

81: Photography by Marlene Wetherell for Ulla Maija

82: Courtesy of Mr. and Mrs. C.P. Dennehy

83: From left: courtesy of Mr. and Mrs. David Bain; right: by John Dolan

84-85: Photography by Lynne Brubaker

86: Photography by Cappy Hotchkiss

87: Photography by John Dolan

88: Courtesy of Chado Ralph Rucci

90-91: Courtesy of Chado Ralph Rucci

93-5: Courtesy of Chado Ralph Rucci

96-97: Photography by Carlo Giorgi for Mr. and Mrs. John Long

98: Courtesy of Mr. and Mrs. G. H. Hovagimyan

99: Photography by Pamela Duffy

100: Courtesy of Mr. and Mrs. Phillip Bruno

102: Photography by Ken Skalksi

103: Photography by Carlo Giorgi for Mr. and Mrs. John Long

104: From top left clockwise: Barry Verner for Mr. and Mrs. William Tracy; photography by Tom Rosenthal; photography by Ken Skalksi

107: Courtesy of Zac Posen

108-109: All pictures courtesy of Zac Posen

110-113: Photography by Marlene Wetherell for Ulla Maija

119: All photography by Carlo Giorgi for Mr. and Mrs. John Long

120: From top left clockwise: photography by Dominic Harvey for Sarah Morris and Jeffrey Michael; photography by Dominic Harvey for Sarah Morris and Jeffrey Michael; photography by Kiriko Shirobayashi for Sarah Morris and Jeffrey Michael

121: All photography by John Dolan

122: All photography by Pamela Duffy

123: Photography by Roxanne Lowit

125: All photography by Peter Hamblin

126: © John Springer Collection / CORBIS

127: Courtesy of Diane Meier Delaney

128: © altrendo images / Getty Images

132: Courtesy of Mr. and Mrs. David Bain

134: All pictures courtesy of Mr. and Mrs. David Bain

136-139: All photography by Cappy Hotchkiss

140: From left: Alison Miller courtesy of David Goodwin; Rosemary Bray McNatt courtesy of Ben Goodwin

141: Photography by Tom Rosenthal

143: Photography by Peter Hamblin

144: Photography by Kiriko Shirobayashi for Sarah Morris and Jeffrey Michael

145: Photography by Chris Danemayer for Sarah Morris and Jeffrey Michael

146: Julia Moburg for Sarah Morris and Jeffrey Michael

149: Illustration by Anne Watkins

150-152: Photography by Lynne Brubaker

154: Courtesy of Mr. and Mrs. Phillip Bruno

155: All pictures courtesy of Mr. and Mrs. Phillip Bruno

156-157: Photography by Pamela Duffy

158-161: All photography by John Dolan

162: Photography by Tom Rosenthal

163: Courtesy of Diane Meier Delaney

166-167: Photography by Carlo Giorgi for Mr. and Mrs. John Long

168-169: All pictures courtesy of Mr. and Mrs. Phillip Bruno

170: Courtesy of Sylvia Weinstock

171: From left clockwise: photography by John Dolan; photography by Lynne Brubaker; photography by Sueraya Shaheen

172-177: Photography by John Dolan

178: From left clockwise: photography by Kiriko Shirobayashi for Sarah Morris and Jeffrey Michael; photography by Paula Huston for Sarah Morris and Jeffrey Michael; photography by Kiriko Shirobayashi for Sarah Morris and Jeffrey Michael

179: Photography by Lynne Brubaker

184: Photography by Tom Rosenthal

185: Photography by Peter Hamblin

186: Photography by Ben Fink for Cupcake Café

187: All photography by Ben Fink for Cupcake Café

188: All photography by Cappy Hotchkiss

189: All photography Lynne Brubaker

190: From left: photography by Peter Hamblin; photography by Tom Rosenthal; photography by Peter Hamblin

191: From top left clockwise: photography by Peter Hamblin; photography by Tom Rosenthal; photography by Peter Hamblin; photography

by Peter Hamblin

192-197: Photography by Peter Hamblin

199-200: Illustration by Anne Watkins

201-202: Courtesy of David Millman

203-204: All illustrations by Anne Watkins

205: Courtesy of David Millman

211: Courtesy of Diana McSpadden and Rick Todd

212-213: All photography by Ken Skalksi

218: Dolan portrait by Holger Thoss for John P. Dolan

219: All photography by John Dolan

220: From top clockwise: Brubaker portrait by Rhea Brubaker for Lynne Brubaker; photography by Lynne Brubaker; photography by Lynne Brubaker; photography by Lynne Brubaker

221: Photography by Lynne Brubaker

222: From top clockwise: Lowit portrait by Jesse Frohman for Roxanne Lowit; photography by Roxanne Lowit

223: All photography by Roxanne Lowit

224-225: Photography by Peter Hamblin

226: Watkins portrait by Julie Skarrett Photography

227: All illustrations by Anne Watkins

229: Photography by Peter Hamblin

232: *From left to right, top row:* courtesy of Mr. and Mrs. Ben Rosen, photography by Pamela Duffy, courtesy of Mr. and Mrs. David Bain; *bottom row:* photography by Tom Rosenthal, photography by Barry Verner, photography by John Dolan

232: *From left to right, top row:* courtesy of Mr. and Mrs. Philip Bruno, photography by John Dolan, photography by Carlo Giorgi; *bottom row:* photography by Lynne Brubaker, photography by Cappy Hotchkiss, photography by Kiriko Shirobayashi

INDEX